The Play of Awakening

*Adventures in Direct
Realization Tantra*

Jaya Kula Press
110 Marginal Way, PMB 196
Portland, Maine 04101
jayakula.org

Cover and interior design and layout: Saskia Nicol
saskianicol.com

Library of Congress Control Number: 2018910071

Sarasvati, Shambhavi

The Play of Awakening: Adventures in Direct Realization Tantra

ISBN:
9781732218321

Printed in the United States of America on acid-free paper.

The Play of Awakening

Adventures in Direct Realization Tantra

Shambhavi Sarasvati

Jaya Kula Press Books

by Shambhavi Sarasvati

Pilgrims to Openness: Direct Realization Tantra in Everyday Life, 2009

The Play of Awakening: Adventures in Direct Realization Tantra, 2012

Returning: Exhortations, Advice and Encouragement from the Heart of Direct Realization Practice, 2015

No Retreat: Poems on the Way to Waking Up, 2016

Nine Poisons, Nine Medicines, Nine Fruits, 2017

The Reality Sutras: Seeking the Heart of Trika Shaivism, 2018

For players of this game

Be intoxicated with, infused in, attached to, engrossed with, and exposed to Him; then only it can be understood that everything in this creation is His manifestation, He Himself, His playground.[1]

—Anandamayi Ma

Contents

Waking Up Together

An introduction to the revised edition of The Play of Awakening

This book is an offering of friendship to anyone on a conscious path of spiritual awakening. It wants to support you in your efforts to discover the wisdom inherent in reality, to warn you of possible detours, and to make you laugh.

My first book, *Pilgrims to Openness*, presents an overview of the tradition of direct realization Tantra, also called Trika Shaivism, Shaivite Tantra, and Kashmir Shaivism. In it, I offer a practical introduction, especially to how everyday life functions as spiritual practice.

This book is aimed at those who have already set out on the kind of path that causes us to experience profound and sometimes unsettling transformations of body, energy, and mind. It looks at many of the nitty gritty circumstances, including the obstacles, that arise when we are engaged in consistent spiritual practice.

I am speaking from my experience as a practitioner in traditions from India and Tibet. However, I hope that this book can be useful to people on a variety of paths.

Many of the teachings published here were originally blog posts. They are written in everyday language and are organized thematically, but loosely. Feel free to skip around, meander, double back, or read straight through.

May it be of benefit.

Lots of love,
Shambhavi Sarasvati
Portland, Maine
2018

A Note on View and Direct Realization

In this book, as in all of my books, you will often encounter the word "View." View teachings help you to understand what your tradition has to say about the aim of spiritual life, the nature of reality, God, getting born, living, and dying. View teachings are the largest context for your participation in a tradition.

View teachings keep your spiritual practice on track and guide you through times when you are in danger of reinforcing your attachments. Sometimes students are instructed to meditate on View teachings.

View teachings are not philosophy. They are living beacons. View teachings actively point us toward what we will come to embody in our own experience through doing spiritual practice. We hear the View. We practice with the View. When we realize, we are said to be "living the View."

Direct realization means using your senses, including your mind, to discover the nature of reality, of the Self. Spiritual traditions from India and Tibet have many names for what I am calling the Self. Some of these are: living presence, essence nature, Shiva-Shakti, primordial nature, your real nature, absolute reality, the natural state, and original wakefulness. While there are differences in View among direct realization traditions, each of these designations expresses the understanding that reality is alive, aware, and full of wisdom.

Direct realization traditions, including Trika Shaivism, Dzogchen, and Chan Buddhism, teach practices such as meditation, mantra, kriya yoga, and ritual. The aim of such practices is to cause karmic obscurations to subside and thereby enhance our capacity, through our senses, to recognize essence nature. Once having recognized our real nature, we continue until we can remain undistracted from that and immersed in that. While this may sound rather technical, the result of recognizing and becoming immersed in living presence is total open-heartedness and unconditional devotion toward all of life's manifestations.

1.
Cutting
Through

The journey toward the discovery of our real nature begins with the loss of concepts about ourselves and spirituality that we once held dear.

Use Everything

Everything we encounter is made of and by the same primordial wisdom. This is the view of direct realization traditions such as Trika Shaivism and Dzogchen. They teach us how to discover our own real nature and the nature of reality directly through our senses and mind.

Because all of life is an expression of an alive, self-aware intelligence, we can use every aspect of life to help us to wake up and discover what and how we really are. We can bring every circumstance onto our path, from cooking a meal to meditating, from unruly emotions to boredom and joy. Everything and everyone can be a vehicle to help us to wake up if we are ready to open our minds, drop our concepts, and let wisdom speak directly to us through circumstance.

We can perform complicated yogic practices or meditate on the moment after a sneeze. We can work with the energy of joy as well as with the energies of jealousy, anger, hatred, fear, and disgust. We can practice while on retreat in a cave as well as while walking in a city park or sitting in a cafe. We can use our relationships, our eating, our movement, our work, and our play as fields of practice and gateways to realization.

To practice in this direct way, we must be willing to be with things just as they are. We must step out of fantasy: out of how we wish to be or wish circumstances to be. We must be willing to feel and encounter the messiness of ourselves and others without embellishment. Our most powerful tools for practice are right here in the unembellished experience of life unfolding.

Akhanda sadhana means "unbroken practice." Doing unbroken practice, we make a continuous effort to remember our real nature and to use the tools of our traditions, especially when we find ourselves sliding comfortably into fixation and reactivity. It takes awareness, courage, confidence, and commitment to pull yourself away from limited habits of body, emotion, and mind over and over again, not just when you are sitting on a meditation cushion, but everywhere.

We must undertake this effort without a complete understanding of the fruits of our effort. No matter what anyone tells us or what we read about spirituality in books, the fruit only becomes visible as we experience it, day-by-day, step-by-step.

This alive, aware reality expresses itself along a continuum of more subtle to more coarse experiences. When I use words such as "coarse" or "gross," I mean the aspects of everyday experience that are more tangible and accessible.

Using whatever is ready-to-hand, we walk backwards, we return. What do we return to? We return to encounter reality and ourselves with more subtle, expansive senses. We return to take refuge in our own unconditioned, unlimited nature. We return to the radical openness of the primordial heart.

Cutting Through

Don't Believe Me, or Anyone

Cutting Through

The living, self-aware world provides human beings with uncountable methods for waking up to the fullness and freedom of our real nature. From simple, devotional acts, such as pouring water on the earth, to complex rituals; from solitary prayer to mantra and meditation, the spiritual practices we encounter in our human realm are natural technologies for waking up. This uneven process leads us inexorably from states of relative ignorance to usable wisdom.

Many spiritual traditions are founded on faith, trust, belief, and hope. These are valuable feeling orientations for people who are attracted to those traditions. In the direct realization traditions, faith, trust, belief, and hope are definite impediments. Students in these traditions are advised to use their minds and their senses to find out for themselves about the nature of reality and to develop confidence in the life process.

The wonder is: we can actually find out. We can find out what we are and how reality works. We can become vastly more skillful in our interactions with the world. We can do this by relaxing our senses, including our minds, until the ways of our lives and our world become directly perceivable, until knowledge of the Self stands revealed.

In order to actually find out, we must become explorers of our own nature, the nature of reality. We must let go of the limited concepts about ourselves and the world that we have come to embody over the years and lifetimes. These repeating habits of limited understanding are our karma.

It's not easy to loosen our attachment to the ways we have always acted, felt, and thought. It takes a certain quantity of energy and courage to open ourselves to experiencing reality in a new, yet profoundly intimate way. All of us need help.

In the direct realization traditions, help comes in the form of a deep relationship with a teacher who has walked the path before us. The teacher's job is to deliver us to a direct, immediate encounter with our real nature. The job of the student is to bravely recognize what is being transmitted through the teacher and to do the work needed to erode the experience of limitation.

Contemporary people often feel that having a close relationship with a spiritual teacher is unnecessary. People hop from one teacher to another, mixing and matching Views and practices from different traditions. This is usually a strategy for preserving small self and its false sense of independence.

In reality, the practice of discipleship is a completely natural phenomenon. The co-arising relationship of teacher and student is the natural technology that Self has manifested in order to enact the play of waking up. What we ultimately discover is that all of reality is expressing devotion to itself and that the teacher-student relationship is a means for discovering that.

Cutting Through

Ambition and Longing

Spiritual ambition is when we use our energy to build up our self-image by striving for results in our spiritual life. For instance, we do our practice with certain goals in mind because we want to be known for having achieved those goals. If we are lucky, we discover that any preconceptions about the outcome of spiritual practice are shaped by our limited condition.

Spiritual longing, on the other hand, is the voice of God. Spiritual longing may cause us to work very hard in our practice, but we will be moving toward the limitless source of that longing, not toward some puny goal invented by small I.

Americans have the ambition *samskara* bad. (A samskara is literally a karmic "scar.") It's hard for us to really, really get it that life is not one long, individualistic effort leading upward and onward to personal and professional glory. If we have one job, we've got our eye on another job. If we aren't looking too publicly successful, we suffer. If someone else knows more, makes more money, or attracts more attention, we experience jealousy and may even attempt to hurt the other person. Or we puff ourselves up extravagantly. We are almost always competing.

Cutting Through

Many people here in the U.S. treat their spiritual practice as yet another ladder of levels to conquer or amazing experiences and powers to acquire. An astounding number of people begin their practice with the idea that they want to be teachers. If they become teachers, they relentlessly pursue money and fame.

Direct realization practice is a method for discovering an extraordinary life. This extraordinary is not something you plan or create. You can't climb the ladder to extraordinariness. This extraordinary is not a career goal. In fact, the compulsive, competitive measuring of spiritual accomplishment causes any potential fruit of our practice to wither and rot on the vine.

The extraordinary we discover was there all along, complete and replete. It is the spontaneous play of all of existence when experienced through more open perception. It is not something you accomplish. In order to realize this, you must totally surrender any contrivance of self or world concept, including preconceptions about the fruits of spiritual life.

The process of letting go of your fundamental defensiveness requires that you follow primordial longing. When you meet an appropriate teacher, practice, and tradition, your longing will in some way recognize the limitless home for which it has been searching. By following the teacher and teachings one step at a time, rather than willfully setting competitive goals in advance, you discover wonder, delight in life, and contentment.

If we hang onto our spiritual ambition, our mad scramble for recognition, and our pre-fabricated goals, we will end up with just more anxiety, disquiet, insecurity, and disease. If we remain dependent on maintaining self-image, we will not be willing to give up what needs to be given up or follow what needs to be followed. Letting go is even harder when careers are entangled with spiritual practice.

In the *Bhagavad Gita*, Lord Krishna teaches that everything a yogi does is *yajña*—a devotional offering. This continual state of offering is exemplified by the mantra *svaha*. Svaha means: I offer my small self to the larger Self, the world Self. This is a description of the life of a real yogi or yogini. Yajña is real yoga.[2]

Being in a state of following and offering does not mean powerlessness. When you offer up your small self, you let go of your identification with your limitations. You begin to relate more consciously to the wisdom and energy of the world Self. The extreme self-referentiality, self-interest, and self-concern that characterizes many people's experience begins to shift toward the spontaneous embodiment of devotion toward all of the creation. It means being in a state of unconditioned responsivity, immersed in the living presence we call reality.

Spiritual ambition takes an enormous amount of energy to maintain. Enormous. Spiritually ambitious people may look like they are surrendering deeply or doing a lot of *karma yoga* (service). They put out big energy, big Shakti. But only a small percentage of that energy ends up nourishing them or the people around them. Most of the energy is syphoned off into maintaining self-image. A person may feel pumped up by the amphetamine of achievements and public recognition. But eventually, exhaustion will take its toll.

Spiritual ambition creates spiritual starvation all around. When you sincerely and bravely follow your longing, no matter where it leads you, the whole "problem" of what to do, how to do it, and what rewards "it" will bring, subsides. With patience, humility, constancy to practice, courage, and sincerity, you will eventually become a fountain of nourishment in every circumstance, large or small.

Cutting Through

Fall Into Emptiness

Shunya is the experience of emptiness we encounter when limited self and world concepts dissolve. For instance, if your house burns down, or your lover leaves you or if some cherished idea you have about yourself is overturned by your spiritual teacher, in that very instant of loss, you can discover shunya.

Shunya is the experience of the gap arising in the moment between a limiting concept being lost or ripped away and our efforts to regroup.

We go around acting as if our house is solid, safe, and at least a semi-permanent refuge for our life. Then, in one hour, the house is burglarized, an earthquake demolishes it, or it burns down. Our concepts about life crash along with it.

Recall a moment such as this: the exact moment when you learned similarly shattering news. You may recall a feeling of profound destabilization, something like free fall. This is the gap. The gap opens us to more reality, to space, to vitality in the form of fear and openness. In this gap, we encounter a direct, embodied, nonconceptual experience of the impermanence of our concepts, objects, and relationships.

If we are not practitioners, we do our best to scramble out of the gap as quickly as possible. We try to replace what has been lost. We try to replace the things and people that gave us the feeling of permanence and safety. We try to "recover" from the trauma of shunya. As practitioners, we want to taste the gap as deeply as possible. We want to yield as completely as possible to the gap.

Many of the practices we do are designed to lead us to let go of limiting concepts of self and world and to experience their insubstantiality. When we have a wrong idea that shunya, or this experience of insubstantiality, is the fundamental nature of reality, we try to hold onto the experience. Then shunya itself becomes a limitation on our self-realization.

The experience of shunya relates to how we feel when some aspect of our limited understanding of reality is destroyed. It is an experience of a transition in our View. It is not the ultimate realization.

If we let go and let the experience of shunya arise and subside naturally, we come into a completely different experience. Reality is not empty: it is full of awareness, vitality, and wisdom. We come into a direct encounter with living presence.

This living presence is made of clarity, intelligence, compassion, devotion, and curiosity. It is both God and our own Self. In order to discover this, we must let our concepts of self and other be stripped away by our daily practice and the encounter with our teachers. We have to fall into emptiness in order to discover fullness.

23

Cutting Through

2.
Setting Out

The desire to practice emerges spontaneously from an infinite mandala of circumstances, all moving you toward the revelation of a deep longing to know what you truly are.

Longing to know the Self

Imagine yourself standing in front of a beautiful Hindu or Buddhist painting depicting teachers and deities. Perhaps hundreds of arms swirl around the deities, each hand curved into a different graceful gesture or brandishing a uniquely fearsome weapon for demolishing limitations. The teachers assume yogic postures, or simply overflow with cosmic compassion. Detailed foliage grows along the borders. The painting is an orchestrated riot of rich mineral colors and luminous gold.

Now focus in on a smaller area of the painting. Move closer. There, another layer of world unfolds. Smaller figures dance within the landscape of color. Tiny Sanskrit mantras weave here and there. A ritual fire, a moon, a river, a yogi, a mountain abode are all rendered in meticulous detail.

Move even closer. Experience the bursting forth of yet another layer of life, another precise world realized in subminiature scale. Discover an entire planet of beings within the shaft of the Devi's hair, or the play of lotuses on the surface of a teardrop-sized lake.

Move closer yet again, and the intricate patterns that make up the complex whole come into view: the crosshatches, shadings, whispers of line and swirl. The infinite fields of grass-like brush-strokes hold multiple layers of creation bound tightly together on one piece of cloth.

Why all of these minute permutations? Why so many worlds within one world? The mandalas of life represented are revelations of reality, born out of the direct insight of yogis and adepts. They are living symbols.

Normally we think of symbols as representing something. For instance, the word "apple" represents a fruit, but we could collectively choose a different word. In contrast, a living symbol is a real expression or aspect of what it represents. The profuse and precise overflowing of Hindu and Buddhist works of art exemplifies the many modes of appearing of the essence nature. We can experience these works of art and directly learn something about how the world really is.

Try it. Look out across a landscape in nature. Take in the scene as one whole, then continually adjust your focus until you are seeing down into the intricate worlds that populate the whole. Doing this, you can have a direct experience that the mandala of the natural world and the mandala of the paintings are born of a single, continuous creative process. You can admire the unreserved, infinitely modulated creativity in both.

You may be aware of your motivations for embarking on a more conscious spiritual path. Many people begin because they want to alleviate some kind of mental, emotional, or physical pain. Others begin because they experience the persistent feeling that life is missing some crucial ingredient not to be found in career, family, or at the mall. Relatively fewer people meet a teacher who inspires and moves them or a tradition that captures their imagination or intellect.

Whatever your reasons are or were, eventually all motivation converges at the desire to know the nature of reality. After all secondary motivations fall away, this single desire is revealed and begins to grow larger and larger in your life.

The desire to know who and what you really are is the same as the desire to know all of reality. The Self, your Self, is pervasive and continuous. Your smaller experience of being a separate individual is a creative expression of the one Self. Hindu and Buddhist art reveals the infinite variety of this overflowing creativity and stimulates wonder and curiosity—two wisdom virtues of the enlightened Self.

The desire to reveal your Self fully to yourself is a natural desire; it is the power or Shakti that drives all beings inexorably toward what we call awakening. The limitations to self-understanding that you now experience are aspects of the play of the world Self hiding and then unveiling its true nature like a cosmic game of peek-a-boo.

As you walk the path of waking up to your own nature, you experience many small enlightenments along the way. Inevitably, you begin to notice more sharply the limitations to your understanding. This is at least somewhat painful, but absolutely necessary. Feeling the pain of being limited is an aspect of self-realization.

Eventually understanding grows, and you discover a strong desire to release these limitations. You understand better now how they restrict your spontaneity and participation in the manifest world.

When some of these limitations begin to relax their grip on you, you express more natural curiosity about other people and the world. You will become motivated by a strong desire to directly perceive and engage with more subtle manifestations of the creation. You may want to learn more about the laws of creation and how to work with them in your everyday life.

When your own nature, the nature of the Self, stands revealed even more, the devotional essence of reality becomes paramount. A more profound and all-encompassing longing for immersion in living, aware presence arises. That longing becomes like a romance with reality that never stops.

Setting Out

Walk Slowly and Remember

What is required of a pilgrim on the Supreme Path is that he should ever keep on walking. To spend one's time in the remembrance of the Eternal does indeed mean to be a traveller on this Path.[3]
—Anandamayi Ma

Students often want to know how to fit spiritual practice into their busy lives. Even if a practice only takes ten or twenty minutes, sometimes people can't decide to do it.

Instead, they may spend years struggling with themselves about doing or not doing. This takes much more energy and time than just sitting down. But at least they are thinking about the world with a bit of a larger View. This is a painful way to progress, but it really is better than nothing.

The only reason we don't go along more easily with the natural process of waking up is because we get distracted by the momentum of our karmic habit patterns. When students ask teachers for advice about how to "fit" spiritual practice into their day, or if they insist that they cannot practice because of other obligations, generally people want strategies for squeezing more into an already overcrowded life.

A student of mine who didn't manage to settle into a regular practice after coming to teachings for a couple of years continually invoked the mantra that he only wanted to "add and not subtract." He was an over-worker and an over-player. He didn't want to give anything up to make room for spiritual practice. This caused him unhappiness, but he wasn't ready to make a change.

The answer to this kind of karmic dilemma is to just to wait until your longing for self-discovery grows stronger. You will eventually reach a tipping point where that longing begins to shift the momentum in your life toward making room for activities that help you to wake up. This is fine, but if you are able to do some practice every day now, you can discover sooner. Why is this important? Because this life in this body is impermanent.

I try to impress on my students that all I do is walk, day by day, putting one foot in front of the other. I just keep practicing. Every day. In this way, any ordinary person such as myself discovers an extraordinary world.

Doing practice of some kind, and remembering God or Guru or your real destination every day is the most important, life-changing thing you can do. When you practice every day, even if it is only for twenty minutes, you begin to remember. You begin to remember who you are. You begin to wake up from the slumber we call normal life.

You will discover more fruit if you practice at the same time every day, and if you remember to be in the state of your practice at other times while you are going about your daily activities. You can recall how you felt when you were done your seated practice and then try to bring that feeling back on in the midst of daily life. You can think of your teacher or God or of your longing for home. You should try to remember.

This is how to practice when you have a full life, but you are ready to let your longing lead you. Over time, longing will grow. Eventually it will become a river of longing that takes you home.

29

Setting Out

Becoming Fully Human

The yearning to discover the full potential of life in a human body is one of the core motivations for undertaking spiritual practice. Right now, you are likely only able to experience a small percentage of your human potential.

Some traditions glorify their teachers as divinities or encourage students to have deities as teachers. In the direct realization traditions, we say it is important to have a human teacher because we are learning how to be human.

My Guru, Anandamayi Ma, was constantly experimenting with the experience of being fully awake in a human body. She could do what we consider to be extraordinary things, such as be in two places at the same time, levitate, or go without food and water. There was never any earnestness or pride connected to these experiments, only a *bhava* (feeling orientation) of playfulness.

Ma was renowned for healing people, reading the thoughts of others, seeing future events, perfectly performing rituals connected with spiritual traditions not her own, invoking mantras and scriptures in languages she had not studied, and generally interacting with reality on the most subtle levels. But most important was her great kindness, compassion, and ability to host all circumstances and people without exception. When I think of the human capacities I most want to embody, it is these.

When we do not have much realization, we divide up the world into family, friends, acquaintances, lovers, and strangers. The latter category includes nearly everyone.

We easily become annoyed with or frightened by others. We find some people to be "crazy," or "weird," and we don't like those people. We are very, very lonely.

More realized people show us that it is possible to live as a human being without being defensive or aggressive. We can relax our tensions and become fountains, showering everyone with compassion. We can love everyone. We don't have to travel to a heaven to do this or become deities. We can do it right here while we are human beings.

As practitioners, we are also preparing for the dissolution of this human form and the completion of at least this particular instance of human embodiment. If we are highly accomplished, we can complete the human experience. This means relaxing so deeply that your karmic entanglements no longer bind you to this form. You are free to go or to stay.

Those who choose to stay are called *jivanmukta* (liberated in life), or *mahasiddha* (greatly accomplished). Such beings bring benefit to everyone simply by choosing to remain among us.

Most of us have extremely limited notions of self-realization. These ideas usually involve visions of the individual self accumulating powers and pleasures without giving up its sense of autonomy and self-importance. Most people find it difficult to envision realization outside of this box of small I.

A student once complained bitterly that doing daily practice was useless because he would eventually die. The strands of karmic patterning that made up his unique individual experience in this lifetime would disperse. Then there would be no "him" to enjoy his accomplishments. So why bother?

This kind of achievement orientation does not care about being of benefit to others. It puts little stock in simply becoming a more skillful, compassionate human being. Mostly, it just doesn't understand that the appearance of students, teachers, and a path is nature expressing itself. It is the cosmic game par excellence. Walking a path of waking up is simply the most fun to be had as a human being.

Self-realization can be understood as being related to freedom. The freedom of this alive, aware reality is unlimited, unconditioned, and playful self-expression. As we wake up, we become more fully and spontaneously expressive. We are not as bound by habit patterns. We are not as reactive to circumstances and other people. We develop more range of expression in our body, energy, and minds.

Along the way, we have to get it that reality is not accomplishing anything other than self-expression. There is no final goal, no ultimate achievement. The spiritual traditions that posit such ultimacy are only God playing at that, even if their adherents don't realize it.

We can only experience freedom of expression when we are in a state of profound nonattachment. If we are not, our expression will not be playful. It will be conditioned by likes and dislikes, by anxieties and specific cravings. We will be serious and self-important.

Actual self-realization is like living in a continual state of improvisation. We have no grand plan, and all goals are functional and short-term. We can respond to life's ever-changing circumstances like surfers adjusting playfully and skillfully to the rise and fall of waves. Day-by-day, we feel less afraid and constrained.

Setting Out

Doubt

Many practitioners fear their own doubt. They think something is wrong if they doubt themselves, their teachers, or the teachings.

Teachers can also discourage students from expressing doubt because the teachers themselves have unacknowledged doubts. Students are sometimes afraid to voice their doubts for fear of reprisal from teachers and other students.

Our own longing for a teacher and teachings can sometimes become an obstacle to the honest exploration of doubts. We want teachings and teacher to be real and useful. We desperately want to wake up and find our true home. Doubts can be viewed as a scary detour.

The open secret is that 99.99 percent of spiritual aspirants experience doubt.

The Kashmiri Guru and adept, Abhinavagupta, taught that doubt is actually a condition of relative openness. If we are either very ignorant or very sure of ourselves, we are not open to learning. Doubt is a soft feeling, although it can be uncomfortable.[4]

Doubt arises when teachers present us with a View that challenges our habitual, fixed concepts about ourselves and others.

When these are skillfully challenged, doubt arises and opens a gap in a limited worldview.

The student feels resistance and then fear and a kind of emptiness. If surrender happens, the gap can become real spaciousness. Now the student can experience being in the immediacy of life and just exploring and discovering rather than protecting and projecting.

Some people experience a kind of habitual worrying about themselves. This is not the kind of doubt I am talking about. Self-referential worrying is an activity, like playing computer games or binge watching, whose purpose is to distract you from experiencing the impermanence and groundlessness of manifest life.

If you use worry in this defensive way, you need to learn that "don't know" is an authentic, honorable, and relaxing place to sit. Just sit and cultivate having contact with the underlying experience that you don't know about yourself, about others, or about what is going to happen. Fear will arise and then eventually subside. Don't run away from the fear or try to fix it. Just let it be.

Over time, you will begin to feel that not knowing in the ordinary way is fine. You will experience authentic relaxation. Accustom yourself to just sitting in the relaxation of "don't know." Now you are directly encountering your real circumstance. You are ready to find out.

Setting Out

3.
Getting
Guidance

Gurus and disciples arise together as one ornament of living presence. Together they are a natural technology for playing the game of revealing the nature of the Self to the Self.

Let's Play Guru and Disciple!

Student and teacher together are a cosmic process: a function or a capacity. One is not separate from the other. Student and teacher are a unified situation.

The student and teacher together are an expression of the cosmic game or play of self-recognition. Individualized experiencers (people, for instance) forget who they really are. Circumstances naturally arise to help them remember. Student-teacher is one of those circumstances. The game of remembering or self-recognition begins!

Instead of thinking of a student and a teacher primarily as people, think of studenting and teachering. Studenting and teachering are dependent. One cannot exist without the other.

What we call a "student" is a person through whom the cosmic capacity for studenting is expressing. What we call a "teacher" is a person through whom teachering flows. In your role as a student, you should often ask yourself: Am I making myself available to studenting? You should work to open to the cosmic process of studenting.

A Guru is available to the world cosmic process of Guru-ing. A great Guru is like a clear and clean river through which teachering becomes available to anyone who steps into that compassionate flow.

A great Guru and a great disciple together, as one process, demonstrate all of the cosmic virtues: all compassion, all intelligence, all equanimity, all curiosity, all creativity, all playfulness. Everyone benefits from coming into contact with a great teacher and disciple.

When you participate wholeheartedly in the cosmic studenting-teachering process, devotion to one teacher ends in your embodiment of natural devotion to all of the creation. The teacher is your gateway to discovering this.

Anandamayi Ma said to her disciples: *You all have wanted it [me] and you have it now. So play with this doll for a little while.*[5]

Mataji is declaring that her manifestation is the responsiveness of the world to itself. She is a "doll," a piece in the cosmic game. Now let's play!

Transmission

Transmission is key to direct realization traditions such as Trika Shaivism and Dzogchen. Transmission is an inherent experience of deeper realization revealed within the student, generally through the medium of a teacher.

Transmission happens through touch, voice, glance, simple proximity, mind-to-mind, and in dreams. Transmission helps students who are still largely bound to dualistic experience find their way back to an experience of greater continuity with life. Whether we talk about the *darshan* (gaze) of the Guru, "getting" *shaktipat* (hands-on transmission), receiving an empowerment, or seeing our original face, all transmission is a gateway to greater participation in reality.

One common misunderstanding is that during transmission, the teacher gives the student energy that the student lacks. This is wrong View. All energy is *the* energy of the body of the totality. It doesn't belong to the teacher any more or less than it belongs to you. However, teachers with some realization do have access to more energy because they are participating in a larger, less individualized body.

What happens in a transmission situation is that the teacher presents you with the possibility of experiencing enlightened qualities of the natural state within yourself. It is something like removing an obstacle or opening you to a shared experience. The relatively more realized state of the teacher acts as a catalyst for you to taste that directly in you.

A teacher may give formal transmission, but transmission is continuously happening when a teacher is highly realized. If you know how to relax and tune in, just being around your teacher in any ordinary moment is of great benefit.

In truth, reality is continuously "transmitting" the natural state. Most people aren't conscious of this due to heavy conditioning. Revealing direct wisdom through transmission is a cosmic capacity that uses particular people and situations as conduits for our benefit.

Why is transmission so important? Because students must recognize and begin to more fully embody the natural state in order to progress in *sadhana* (spiritual practice). Through transmission, teachers give students tastes of the fruit of sadhana so that students can remember and work toward that. With transmission, you can begin practice with some embodied understanding, not just conceptual knowledge. You know where you are headed.

39

Getting Guidance

Guru Yoga

The relationship to the teacher is the central practice in direct realization traditions. In the mirror of your teacher's greater freedom of expression, you see all of your karmic limitations. In the mirror of the teacher's wisdom and compassion, you see your enlightened, eternal essence nature.

Direct realization traditions offer a huge number of practices you can do: ritual, mantra, hatha yoga, kriya yoga, yantra, and mandala. But in the end, it all comes down to what is called *Guru Yoga*. Guru Yoga is a set of practices through which you can recognize that the enlightened essence of Guru is the same as your own.

In the *Kularnava Tantra*, Lord Shiva says:

He who makes one know: 'I am the knower of the essence of all the Vedas, I am the heart, who is inseparable from God and who is ever-pleased in heart' – he is the Guru.[6]

The Guru is not apart from you existing only to be externally worshipped. Guru is a pervasive function throughout reality. The Guru function, in the form of a human teacher or in another form, helps you to know the continuity of consciousness and energy, the continuity of the Self. Through transmission, or the natural alchemy of the Guru-disciple experience, you discover that the wisdom and virtue at the heart of reality is who you are.

The simplest form of Guru Yoga is to constantly remember your teacher. If your teacher is capable of reflecting essence nature to you, when you are around them, you will feel something special in yourself. By remembering Guru, you can bring on that special feeling of relaxation and spaciousness wherever you happen to be and in any situation.

Try to be in a state of constant remembrance of your Guru. If you have a mantra given to you by that teacher, try to do it while out and about, especially when you are in a stressful situation with another person.

Keep your Guru's face and words and teachings with you at all times. Saturate yourself in their way of being, their state of realization. Feel that you are taking refuge in your true home. Ask for help when, inevitably, your karmic fixations win the day. If you do this, little by little, over time, the qualities of clarity, compassion, and devotion will be revealed in you naturally.

There are more complicated or formal types of Guru Yoga, but they all serve the same function. They all help you to recognize and begin to embody more of your real nature through the gateway of your relationship with Guru.

Upon learning that Guru Yoga is the central practice of direct realization traditions, the eyes of some people glaze over. Ears shut down. Skepticism sets in, even resentment. Most of the contemporary re-inventions of spiritual traditions from Asia involve either the importation of psychological models of the self or the substitution of community or "inner" Guru for a real-life teacher.

In my experience, most of the people who reject living teachers and claim that they are following what they call "inner Guru," or who say "the whole world is my Guru," are beginners on the path. They are just not ready to give up what they erroneously feel is their independence. Inner Guru is not common sense or what feels good

41

Getting Guidance

to you. The true Guru will destabilize your self-concept and challenge your common sense ideas about everything. How many of us will be able to do this work without an expert human guide?

When you are directly accessing Guru without the aid of a human teacher, you will understand the grace and beauty of the phenomenon of Guru. You won't complain about or denigrate true teachers. In fact, the opposite will be true: you will be suffused with wonder and gratitude that teachers exist at all. And you will compassionately desire all beings to feel the grace of Guru raining down on them.

A human Guru is a manifestation of *Guru Tattva*. Tattva means "element" or "function." Guru Tattva is the pervasive element of cosmic wisdom energy that moves us toward self-realization. While it is absolutely true that Guru can be recognized in anything, the human Guru is a naturally arising phenomenon that most people find easier and more effective to relate to during the many stages of waking up.

The primary function of Guru is to serve as a mirror in which we can recognize ourselves. The mirror can manifest in many different ways because a Guru will do anything to help us self-realize. Sometimes "anything" is painful. However, a true Guru is not being mean or authoritarian to satisfy their own needs. What really moves us about a true Guru is their great compassion.

Looking into the face of the infinite compassion and playfulness of Guru, all of our limitations *and* our infinite potential become clear. In the presence of Guru, we can sense the distance between our state of contrivance and the uncontrived natural state. This distance seems simultaneously very far and no distance at all because Guru is showing us our own essence nature.

In the presence of Guru, the destination of our longing reveals itself. At the same time, Guru is not a savior. In the presence of Guru, we discover total responsibility for our condition. We look at Guru, and we know, "this is what I truly am." We know that only we ourselves can take the steps needed to relax our tensions and open to life. Guru shows us this in the mirror of Guru.

It is possible to be in the presence of a great Guru and not recognize this. A human Guru cannot force anyone to look into the mirror. They can only be that for certain people. A person's recognition of Guru is an exquisitely-timed cosmic event occurring within a mandala of circumstances.

Many people have teachers, but they have not met Guru. Their relationship with their teacher is ordinary. This is fine. A person goes along, learning many useful things and growing, but their world has not yet been fundamentally and irrevocably altered.

Meeting and recognizing Guru is a cataclysmic event in the life of a person, even if it is a quiet cataclysm. At this moment, you will become conscious of the fact that all of your pretenses—your decisions, analyses, doubts, worrying, and problematizing—are just so much dust in the wind. You will still keep trying to build a life out of that dust, but somewhere inside, you will already know it is futile.

You will recognize that the expanded state of the Guru is your real destination. And despite the waxing and waning of your resistances and doubts, you will know with certainty that you will eventually come home.

The recognition of the inevitability of self-realization is one of the most shattering and relieving aspects of what one learns by looking in the mirror of Guru. We feel shattered because we know that our attachments will fall by the wayside, and we are not quite ready to let go. We are profoundly relieved because we finally know what we are and that we cannot be left behind.

43

Getting Guidance

The Precise Words of My Teacher

The communicative precision of the primordial Self expresses itself everywhere, but we often encounter this most fully in the words and actions of accomplished teachers. Students will often say how mysterious it is that teachers should speak, without being asked, about exactly what students want to hear in some moment. But most of the time, the teacher is not reading your thoughts!

The open state of the teacher allows for more cosmic "bandwidth." The teacher's words are able to simultaneously address the concerns of many students even though students are in differing conditions. The teacher's words emerge naturally and spontaneously in response to the situation of whoever happens to be around. This is an important lesson that the Guru spontaneously teaches us about how reality works.

Many of my teachers have been exceptionally precise with words. Anandamayi Ma was a consummate communicator. She was able to speak in ways that simultaneously touched people in extremely different circumstances, from the illiterate to the pandit, from the ignorant to the accomplished siddha. She spoke, and still speaks to us, across space and time.

Reality communicates precisely through great teachers, but students, in general, do not yet have the capacity to be precise listeners. When we are relatively ignorant, i.e., stuck in duality, we tend to paint the world with the broad strokes of our concepts and fears. We want a manageable world, a familiar world that we can grasp as easily as possible. We project our desires onto the world instead of listening and letting it communicate to us in its own way.

Many people, upon listening to the precise words of the teacher, have a tendency to turn those words into something familiar, even if that is painful. We may feel happy thinking that we hear the teacher affirming our pet fixations. Or we may become upset because the teacher has said something at odds with our worldview. In many cases, our fears and insecurities cause us to imprecisely listen to the teacher's words or to be unable to digest a new perspective.

At the same time, because we have agreed to be in a teaching situation, we slowly begin to experience more of the picture. After hearing the same thing repeatedly, the real import of the words begins to sink in. At other times, of course, words are heard immediately, and the opening is immediate.

Anandamayi Ma compared the flow of the words of the wise to water dripping on stone. Eventually, the water creates a hole.

By listening repeatedly to discussions and discourses on topics of this kind, the path to first-hand knowledge of what has been heard gradually opens out. You know, it is as when water uninterruptedly dripping on a stone finally makes a hole in it, and then a flood may suddenly surge through which will bring Enlightenment.[7]

Receiving transmission teachings about your real nature is relaxing. Holding onto your fixations and ideas about the world is a lot of work. When you let your concepts and fixations go, it is as if a heavy knapsack has dropped from your shoulders. You can put down your burdens and rest.

The way to receive the transmission of the precise words of a teacher is to relax and open all of your senses. Don't use your legal mind or your emotional drama mind. Listen in a total way. Let yourself be moved. Don't worry about not understanding all of the teachings the first time around. If you just relax, whatever needs to sink in will do that.

Arguing with the teacher is, of course, the path that some people take. And arguing is sometimes, but not always, an aspect of listening closely. Any path is OK, as long as there is also a conscious kernel of willingness to follow your innate desire for realization. In order to realize the fruits of a student-teacher situation and receive the teacher's precious, precise words, any fixation has to be tempered by a certain level of aware responsiveness to this simple, heartfelt desire.

Guru Kula

Most direct realization teachers accept relatively few students with whom they work intensively. This was true in ancient times, and it is still often true today. Not many students are ready for a full-on teacher-student relationship. Human teachers have limitations. They usually cannot provide this function to very many students.

Each teacher-student relationship is unique, and each student requires individualized sadhana and close supervision. In order for the natural technology of teacher-student to work its best magic, teachers and students live in close proximity, usually for years. This is called the *Guru Kula* system. Students become members of the teacher's extended family.

The practice of having daily contact with your teacher is *tapas*, or austerity. It supercharges your practice, continually confronts you with your fixations, and helps you to relinquish tensions via the immersion plan.

Students who have more fully discovered the desire to self-realize do everything possible to remain in the presence of their teachers. Others come and go, regularly escaping to more manageable circumstances, away from the gaze of the teacher and the fire of transmission.

Sometimes teachers have one or a few students, and that is all. More commonly, especially these days, is that teachers have numbers of "come and go" students and only a few for whom they function as Guru, if they are qualified to do that. The heart of the tradition is still teachers working one-on-one with students and finding a way home.

Guru is Different from Teacher

Getting Guidance

Teachers abound, and how wonderful that is! Throughout the course of our lives, we encounter many people who serve as teachers for us. In fact, every person and every life situation can potentially be a teacher. However, teacher is not necessarily Guru.

When we learn a skill or a craft from someone, that person is our *upaya* teacher. The definition of upaya is "skillful means." For instance, most yoga teachers in the West are upaya teachers. They are able to impart some techniques, but they do not have much realization. Most of the teachers we encounter in schools and workplaces are upaya teachers.

You also hear people say: My cat is my Guru, or my children are my Gurus. In most cases, cats and children are not highly realized beings. But we can see things about ourselves and learn from looking in the mirror of our relations with anyone. This mirroring function is an important aspect of a real Guru-student relationship. The difference is that with a real Guru, the mirror is fully awake.

You can also encounter *upaya* Gurus. These are people with some degree of realization from whom you receive particular practices. But you are not relating to that person more broadly as your spiritual preceptor.

The word "Guru" means "dispeller of darkness" and "heavy." Limited View, or ignorance of one's real nature, is the only darkness. The Guru is someone who is willing to do some heavy lifting in order to aid you in dispelling limited View.

In the Guru Stotram, the disciple sings: *Salutations to that glorious Guru who, when I was blinded by ignorance, applied medicine and opened my eyes.* The "medicine" is the transmission and the teachings. The Guru helps you to see in the largest sense. They show you the way to open all of your senses, including your eyes and your mind, so that you can participate in your life with the most exquisite, expansive subtlety.

The Guru is heavy because they keep insisting on prodding, pushing, and poking you to relax your limitations. You want to relax and you don't want to relax, both at the same time. The Guru's "help" can feel very heavy at times. But you should always be aware of the Guru's compassion, no matter how heavy the going gets.

Anandamayi Ma, upon being told that her eyes were causing total devastation to people who encountered her, responded: *Am I really causing total devastation? If you people really underwent a total devastation, that would be something extremely good.*[8]

Guru is a function, a technology, a gateway, and a mirror. Guru is the Supreme Self manifesting as a person in a way that allows less realized people to experience that Supreme Self as themselves. If you are a little bit open, you will notice that being around a Guru feels different from being around other people. It may be somewhat shocking or at least unnerving. You will definitely feel moved and answered in a way you have been longing to be answered.

I remember a teaching given by Khenpo Tsultrim Gyamtso Rinpoche that I attended early on in my life as a Tantrika. The state of Rinpoche was so expansive, all of my tensions were painfully highlighted against the backdrop of his greater realization. I was in a kind of "transmission shock," receiving both greater awareness

Getting Guidance

of my fixations and a river-like transmission of the enlightened condition of the teacher. I only spent a few hours with Rinpoche, but the experience flung open the door for me to more embodied understanding.

Seducing the Guru

We are rightly concerned about teachers who seduce their students. At the same time, nearly every student is constantly trying to seduce the teacher.

How do students seduce the teacher? Any following forms of conduct can be deployed for purposes of seduction.

Displaying a lot of knowledge.

Displaying charming ignorance.

Asking interesting questions.

Waiting patiently.

Waving the banner of our courage.

Waving the banner of our anger.

Waving the banner of our sincerity.

Waving the banner of our "correct" View.

Waving the banner of our desperation.

Waving the banner of our devotion.

Waving the banner of our spiritual accomplishments.

Waving the banner of our humility.

Joking around.

Seriousness.

Listening to the teacher a certain way.

Looking at the teacher a certain way.

Favors and service rendered to the teacher, the teacher's family, or the teacher's top students.

Anything we do to be number one.

Serving humbly as number two with the intent of proving we are superior to number one.

Gossiping to the teacher about other students.

Ostentatiously giving gifts to the teacher.

Secretly giving gifts to the teacher.

Flirting with the teacher.

Having sex with the teacher.

Challenging with criticism.

Challenging with difficult "problems."

Challenging with the teachings of other teachers.

Agreeing with the teacher.

Ostentatiously doing spiritual practice in public gatherings where the teacher is present.

Wowing the teacher with amazing dreams.

Wowing the teacher with amazing experiences.

Wowing the teacher with amazing coincidences.

Lying to the teacher.

Rejecting the teacher, but not going away.

Leaving and coming back repeatedly.

Outrageous conduct.

Perfect conduct.

Dissolute conduct.

Anything we do to be noticed.

Anything we do to be noticed not needing to be noticed.

When you try to seduce the teacher, you make the teacher ordinary. You are asking the teacher to support your fixations instead of to assist you in relaxing them. This is what people do in just about every relationship. This is what we call "compatibility." I'll support your fixations if you support mine.

The important thing is to notice, over time, all the ways in which you are trying to seduce the teacher. Every time a seduction works, you feel a little pleasure, but that is just small I getting its fix. This repeated, limited pleasuring reinforces dualistic vision. Karmic momentum gathers strength. You will always need another shot of seduction.

When you catch yourself in the act of seduction, recognize that pattern and relax. In each moment, you can throw off your habit pattern like shrugging off a jacket or shawl. At first, the karmic pattern doesn't stay "off" for very long. But over time, the moments of relaxing add up, and the pattern can resolve naturally.

Getting Guidance

The Only Nice Guru is a Dead Guru

Getting Guidance

Lots of people claim dead Gurus as their root or Satguru. Swami Sivananda of Rishikesh, Ramana Maharshi, Anandamayi Ma, Ramakrishna and Neem Karoli Baba are favorites of the dead Guru set. This is somewhat of a tradition, and it seems to be even more prevalent in India.

Add to this the more recent phenomenon of the world-itinerant Guru. Many teachers now travel incessantly around the globe, hitting each location for only a day or two. A student might see her Guru only once a year, or even less frequently. Just enough time to get a bit of instruction. During the other 364 days, one is free to dream up feel-good fantasies.

By and large, people with dead or absent Gurus are in greater danger of remaining wrapped up in the illusion and delusion that preserves small I's sense of separation and feeds karmic habit patterns.

How can you discern if this is your situation?

If your dead Guru never scares you, confuses you, pisses you off, makes you cry with frustration, or electrifies you with self-recognition, you are not in a Guru-disciple relationship. Dead or alive, near or far, a true Guru is a mirror in which you can clearly and terrifyingly see the degree to which you are caught up in the tensions of "me, myself, and I."

Even the open flow of compassion you experience through your Guru comes with a hint of the terrifying. Why? Because the oceanic compassion of Guru sweeps away all concepts, all safe bunkers of self-limiting ideas.

No more Hallmark versions of love or New Age self-serving "bliss." The Satguru shows us what is possible in the context of a human life, and it is so much more than anything we can imagine. Guru penetrates us with the immeasurable.

The Satguru answers our longing so fully, we discover the cosmic nature of that longing. You might cry like a baby upon hearing reality's answer to its little child, but it will be a cry so simple and complex, so complete and inadequate, so full of wonder, relief, and despair, so utterly paradoxical, there will be no way to tell stories about it later on.

If, in your relationship with your dead Guru, you are always in a state of nice, comfortable, blissed-out bhakti, or ordinary and equally comfortable rationalization, you can be sure that a healthy dose of self-delusion is still at play. A person who functions as a real Guru for us radically opens our hearts so we can discover the limitless heart of this alive, aware reality.

The Guru's compassion is both tender and fierce. Not knowing the fierce aspect of compassion means, for most of us, that we will not find the strength to recognize our real condition.

The Guru's compassion is utterly personal and utterly impartial. It exactly meets our unique situation, yet flows equally for all. For this reason, a Guru can never be bargained with or seduced.

Not recognizing or knowing the impartial aspect of compassion means that we will not open to unconditional compassion. Our expression of compassion will remain limited and self-motivated.

Discovering the Guru, meeting the opportunity of Guru, is

discovering the ineffable something for which you have always longed but could never name. You may want to throw yourself at your Guru's feet, fall into your Guru's arms, and run away all at the same time.

Whatever your Guru says or does and whatever your reaction, even in the midst of seeming to reject what your teacher is showing you, you will know without a doubt that you are being delivered to the truth of your situation. The Guru is an explosion of reality in your body, your mind, and your heart.

This explosion may be noisy and dramatic or nearly imperceptible. But nonetheless, it is a situation of tremendous dynamism. You find yourself deeply moved. You cannot help but tremble at times with both fear and relief.

A teacher is chosen after due consideration. You do not choose a Guru. Guru is not a decision. Guru is a sudden discovery of Self.

The world presents us with infinite possibilities for self-realization. So why not a dead Guru or far-away Guru? If a student is capable of meeting the ever-present, pervasive phenomenon of Guru in this form, why not?

Guru operates irrespective of space and time. Guru is focalized through a human being, but it is not contained by that human being. However, recognize that to meet reality in the mirror of a Guru who is no longer in a human body and sharing our everyday lives requires tremendous determination, longing for reality, subtlety of perception, and discernment.

A friend of mine who is a direct disciple of Anandamayi Ma told me that he feels it is easier for those disciples who never met her because they do not have to encounter the Guru's personality. They only perceive her "pure" form. This is a misunderstanding. Human personality is also an expression of this alive, aware reality. Dealing with your reactions to the Guru's personality is an important part of your sadhana.

Guru's function is to aid us in seeing ourselves with total clarity.

We see both our full potential and our reactivity reflected in the mirror of Guru. A fantasy relationship cannot do this work for us. Most of us need the phenomenon of Guru in our lives, up close and personal, showing us the way.

Where's my Guru?

Meeting any true teacher, recognizing that encounter, and being able to take a certain amount of nourishment from it, in general means that you have cultivated the conditions for this to occur. Cultivation means your own efforts to wake up from the slumber we call normal human existence. You feel a certain quantity of desire to know yourself and your world on a level that is not so ordinary.

Another person might hear of a teacher and think that sounds interesting. But if they do not yet have feel desire to self-recognize, it is likely that they will not go to meet the teacher.

Maybe the teacher is 1,000 miles away, or 100, or only a few, but that won't matter. Something will always seem to be in the way. I don't have the money or the time. It's raining outside. I'm tired. I can't find a babysitter. My partner won't like it. I already have plans. A reasonable sounding reason will always take precedence.

Or maybe someone meets a good teacher, but the teacher does not match up with the person's concept of what a teacher is supposed to be and how a teacher is supposed to act. The person feels a little uncomfortable around the teacher and automatically thinks something is wrong because of that. Many people assume that they should only feel comfort and pleasure when they are around spiritual teachers and when they do spiritual practice.

All this means is that someone is not ready for Guru. A person who is ready will be willing to explore the possibility that their own concepts about self and world are the cause of their suffering. They will be open to having these concepts challenged. This person will go to meet the teacher no matter what.

Another circumstance can arise in which a person *does* recognize the special movement of wisdom energy between themselves and a teacher, but it scares them to such a degree that they stay away. This happened at first between Ramakrishna and his principle disciple Vivekananda. Vivekananda was also a bit put off by Ramakrishna's wild style. Ramakrishna's way of showing up just did not fit Vivekananda's idea of teacher.

Meeting your Guru is a total cosmic situation. You are meeting your own Self reflected to you by another in a special way that you can recognize. A person has to be ready for this to occur.

Who is ready for every cherished self-concept and limitation to be pointed out, shown up for what it really is, and relentlessly hunted down? Only those whose natural desire to self-realize has begun to reveal itself.

So, the short answer to the question "Where is my Guru?" is another question. *Where are you?* What are you willing to do to receive teachings? Are you ready to allow your self-concepts to be dismantled? Is your desire strong enough?

4.
Sitting Down

Sitting every day for practice reveals our current condition and all that we have always been but have forgotten.

The Whoomph Factor

When we feel sadness or frustration or pain, we often feel badly about these feelings. We equate feeling good with success and feeling badly with failure. So we feel pain, and we feel ashamed of our pain. We concoct all sorts of activities and thought remedies to try to numb the pain and the shame of pain.

When we feel happy or in some moment our life seems to have meaning and importance, we feel we want to prolong this state. Lurking in the background is the knowledge that we surely won't be able to prolong it, but we think we should be able to if we could just get it right. So we concoct all sorts of activities and thought remedies to try to prolong happiness and stave off its opposite.

We are constantly on guard. We are on guard against failure and disappointment. And we are on guard for happiness, success, and approval. We feel threatened when we allow ourselves, even for a moment, to understand that our happiness is never complete or lasting.

When we begin a seated practice, we carry this pervasive sense of threat with us. Engaged in the simplicity of sitting, most of us cannot help but become the anxious watcher.

Are we doing it right? Are we feeling it right? Are we getting the results? How fast are we getting the results compared to others? Ah... a moment of peace. I'm doing well. I'll try to preserve that good result. Uh oh, here come the bad thoughts again. I'm doomed.

Jetsunma Tenzin Palmo, one of the first Western women to become a Buddhist nun, spent twelve years in retreat in a cave high up in the Himalayas. She wrote that after twelve years in solitude, there was no aspect of herself that had not made itself known to her.[9]

We have many concepts about what seated practice is supposed to bring us: from peace and bliss to boredom and physical discomfort. Despite these ideas, when we begin a consistent, daily, seated practice, everything that we are will show itself sooner or later. Everything that can be experienced *will be* experienced.

If we are physically stiff, we will hurt. If we are anxious and afraid, we will feel restlessness and terror. If we have squashed our natural liveliness with fantasy and overstimulation, we will feel boredom. If we are angry, we will find something or someone to be angry at. If we are sad, we may be overwhelmed by sadness. If we are seeking peace, we will surely encounter it, along with frustration and disappointment. If we desire approval and realize that we are alone, we may feel bitterness and grief. Every little noise may seem amplified and unbearable.

Many people, finding that states of peacefulness or simple relaxation come and go, decide that their practice is "not working." If they are uncomfortable, either physically or emotionally, they feel a sense of failure. Perhaps they even abandon their practice because it doesn't immediately bring the good feelings they expected. They cannot sustain a seated practice because of these limiting concepts and because the fear of naked self-encounter is too great.

Seated practice is a time and space given for us to encounter life expressing itself in all of its richness. Here we can meet ourselves as we really are. We can begin to notice the ways in which we have

63

Sitting Down

used numbing out and frantic activity to muffle our awareness and true longing.

We can also begin to experience contact with the larger liveliness and awareness that holds all of us, without exception, in a compassionate, loving crucible. We can begin to relax and eventually come to laugh at the devices and ruses we employ to escape reality.

I call this beginning phase of practice "the whoomph". We all need to go whoomph. We must take our seat in our real situation without hype or adornment. From this seat in our actual experience, we can begin to wake up.

As in all direct realization spiritual practice, you are an investigator of your real situation. Try to approach whatever discomfort arises with curiosity and discernment and without judgment. View the emotions and sensations that arise as opportunities for discovering greater skill, openness, and awareness.

Our physical pains and emotions are not shameful. They are not merely obstacles. All obstacles, if traversed wisely, result in greater wisdom. Everything here is made of wisdom, and wisdom can be discovered via any circumstance.

One wisdom we should learn is that a good practice is the one that you do. We should remove obvious impediments to doing our practice.

With this in mind, you can use your discernment to take appropriate action given your real condition in that moment. You may decide to shut a window if there is excessive street noise. You may alter your diet and exercise so that you can sit with greater comfort and without so much fidgeting. You might go to bed earlier so that you are fresher in the morning. You might rearrange a work schedule or renegotiate childcare arrangements with your partner.

You may try several meditation cushions before finding the right one. If you have structural obstacles to sitting on the floor, you might decide to sit in a chair. A stoic, heroic attitude is no less self-judging than indulging habitual feelings of failure and inadequacy.

You may find that you have the wisdom and courage to keep sitting, continually and gently returning to the practice at hand, even in the midst of distracting thoughts and emotions. When we are swept away by karmic conditioning, our attitude toward ourselves should be like that we would have toward training a beloved puppy.

Everything that comes up in your seated practice is appropriate to your real situation. There is no threat. You need not reject or grab onto anything. You need not guard against anything other than falling into and remaining in a state of fantasy. Even that is nothing to judge. When you finally notice you have been lost in thought, just refresh your awareness and continue with your practice. Only by continuing on in this practical and tender way will you enjoy the full opportunity to discover what's actually here. Whoomph.

Seating Your Prana and Getting Started

People experiencing busy mind or anxiety sometimes say: I should learn meditation! But meditation is not always the most useful practice in this situation. If the mind is too busy, you may not be able to fruitfully engage in a relatively formless practice. You might have to recalibrate your system and achieve greater balance. Then entering into the state of meditation becomes more possible.

If your mind and emotions are in turmoil, the first place you want to look for recalibration is to your food, movement, and daily routine. Our thoughts and emotions are energy. They are very much affected by what we eat and how we live.

The process of calming down and gaining more equanimity in our basic experience is called "seating the prana." Prana, in this case, means our internal winds. Before we can sit, our prana must sit! When your mind, body, and subtle channels are windy, your spiritual practice will be disturbed.

Routine is the number one medicine for soothing and organizing internal winds. If you eat, sleep, work, play, and move more appropriately, you will gain much more peace of mind than you will struggling to sit and meditate before you are ready.

Good routines to establish are: doing a daily hatha yoga practice, eating appropriate foods at regular times, and infusing your day with the feeling of ritual. The Ayurvedic practice of *dinacharya* can help with ritualizing your activities. Dinacharya means "daily conduct." It is an ancient and healthy protocol for waking up in the morning and conducting yourself during the day. Consulting an Ayurvedic practitioner or a reliable book about Ayurveda is your first step toward learning dinacharya.

For many students, mantra practice is a good place to begin after the prana has calmed down a bit. *Mantra japa* (mantra repetition), is tangible and generally enjoyable. It engages your mind, your energy, your senses, and your body. This helps to further reorient distracted senses and recalibrate them.

Some mantras are universal in that they may be practiced with good result even if you do not have mantra initiation. These are mantras such as *Om*, *Om Namo Narayani*, *Om Nama Shivaya* and *Om Ma*.

If you are practicing one of these mantras without the guidance of a teacher, you should do your best to learn the correct pronunciation. You can ask a person who knows Sanskrit or try to find a reliable recording. You can find recordings of public mantras on the Jaya Kula website.

I would not recommend learning these mantras, or any mantra, from a kirtan recording. Mantras sung in kirtan have a different intonation than the same mantras used for japa practice.

The best way to get a mantra is to receive it from a teacher who has realized the wisdom of the mantra. Realizing the wisdom of the mantra is called "piercing" the mantra. If a teacher has pierced the mantra, then they will be able to transmit the mantra to you in a more activated form.

If you receive a mantra from a teacher via initiation, you should practice the mantra exactly as it is given to you. Even if the pronunciation is different from what you have heard elsewhere, you should do it as your teacher instructs. The mantra your teacher gives you

67

Sitting Down

is the form of the mantra they have realized, not some other sound.

One time, a teacher of mine transmitted a powerful healing mantra. It was in Sanskrit, but the words were pronounced in the Tibetan way. This is quite different from how the same mantra would be pronounced by a teacher from India. I had to record my teacher chanting the mantra so that I could learn his pronunciation exactly and unlearn the "correct" pronunciation.

At a later retreat, the teacher was angry because some people had complained about his pronunciation of the healing mantra. He gave it again, this time pronouncing it in perfect university Sanskrit. But his icy tone of voice made me suspect that this was not the real mantra!

Another answer about how to pronounce a mantra is illustrated by this story. A certain person had been a yogi in a former life, but in order to resolve some karma, in his present life he was a simple, uneducated farmer.

One day, the farmer heard monks chanting a mantra. It was a mantra the farmer had practiced a lot in his former life, but of course he didn't remember this now. However, he felt attracted to the mantra, so he started to chant it as best he could, pronouncing it in some funny way.

Day after day, plowing up and down his fields, the farmer constantly chanted the mantra. As years went by, the farmer and his family prospered. The farmer became more and more peaceful and expansive in his view. Although he was uneducated in this life, he began to remember some of the wisdoms he had previously learned, and so he became a respected person in his community.

One day, a scholar walked by the farm and heard the farmer chanting the mantra as he plowed his field. The scholar addressed the farmer saying: *You are pronouncing that mantra incorrectly, you ignoramus!* The farmer felt ashamed. He begged the scholar to teach him the correct pronunciation. This made the scholar feel important. He arrogantly gave the farmer the corrected mantra.

Sitting Down

More time went by, and the farmer's life again had changed, but this time for the worse. His crops were failing. He and his family became poor, and the farmer no longer gave such wise advice to his neighbors.

Now the scholar happened to come by again. He heard the farmer, doggedly repeating the "correct" mantra, and he saw that the conditions of the farmer's life had changed. He realized his mistake and immediately asked the farmer to go back to his old way of pronouncing. The farmer happily did so, and his life prospered again.

This story illustrates that when fate, grace, diligence, and devotion align in a person's life, all bets are off. Anything can be accomplished

A Conversation with Bodies and Time

Sitting Down

Although many of us have forgotten this, the entire manifest world is a time piece. Our mechanical (or digital) watches are a pale reminder of the inexorability of the life process. Stars, planets, seas, and our own bodies go tick tock, tick tock.

Our bodies converse continuously with natural cycles of living and dying, waxing and waning, creating and destroying, expanding and contracting, revealing and concealing. When we don't live by these natural cycles, our bodies slowly start to forget the correct vocabulary and develop their own sociopathic language. I must have caffeine. I can't eat until afternoon. I'll just lie on the couch for another month. I can't sit still. Another beer! Another 80 hour work week!

Most of the substances Westerners call "medicine" are designed to antidote the ill effects of living out of sync with natural time. Some are designed to override natural time with chemical invincibility. But sadly, the energy we expend in trying to step out of natural time is our own.

When we take a medicine that suppresses illness so that we can work without resting; when we live at the same breakneck pace, regardless of our condition or the season; when we allow our bodies to be anesthetized and cut into for the sake of cosmetic beauty; when we have mechanical sex and remain in depleting friendships, the energy that is being wasted is our own life force. We sink ourselves deeper into energetic debt and move closer to death by exhaustion.

Paradoxically, we strive to look youthful until we die, but we expect to die of disease. When someone dies, our inevitable question is: What did they die of? We can't imagine a death that is not brought on by decrepitude.

Our relationship to illness is truly perverse. We live in a soup of chemical pollutants and radiation of various sorts. We take medicines with debilitating side effects as a matter of course. And yet most of us are desperate to avoid illness.

All of my teachers and the ancient scriptures of my traditions advise that we should take care of our bodies. To be born with a human body is precious because our bodies have the capacity to do many different kinds of sadhana. Our bodies, energy, and minds contain everything we need to realize. Within ourselves, we contain maps for doing practice, maps of the creation, and gateways to pristine wisdom.

We should take care of our bodies in the best way possible for us in our unique circumstances. We will surely not be in perfect health at all times. Some of us will experience chronic illness or disability. But we can work with our bodies in ways that help us to release karma and relax and die with more awareness and energy. This means establishing eating and movement practices that are aligned with your constitution and the seasons. It means becoming knowledgeable about a naturopathic system of daily self-care, such as Ayurveda.

If you care for yourself, your subtle channels will open to more wisdom. You will become more sensitive to your body, energy, and mind; to the seasons; and to the textures of time itself. You will become more skillful in relating to disease and the process of dying.

Sitting Down

Healthy or ill, accomplished human beings support their own and others' unfoldment by caring for their bodies.

Listen to your body. Eat when you are hungry. Eat non-toxic foods to the best of your ability. Rest when you are ill or tired. Support your constitution by consulting a doctor who practices in one of the world's wisdom traditions. Live according to the rhythm of the days and the seasons. Learn to feel time and adapt to changing circumstances. Don't let our stumbling, out of sync culture drag you along with it to chronic depletion and death by exhaustion. This is not the direct realization way.

For many contemporary people, it is a great adventure to rediscover that our bodies are in living relationships with all of reality. Waking up to one's conversation with time is like regaining your senses a thousand fold. You can start on this great adventure now by taking simple, practical steps in your everyday life.

Spiritual Commitments and Vows

People in many traditions take vows. Vow-taking powerfully orients us toward the accomplishment of the vow. Vow-taking creates momentum. In some traditions, people take hundreds of vows. The keeping of vows is in fact their main practice.

Once, I was instructed in a dream not to take any more vows. My flesh and blood teacher instructed me otherwise, and that got me contemplating the whole vow phenomenon. I had a feeling back then that the only authentic vows were those that had somehow already been made, but I didn't really understand my own intuition.

Later, I experienced what might be called "vow events." These were spontaneous vows, made and accomplished simultaneously. In those moments, I recognized a few things about vows.

Vows are open communications. When we are in a state of open communication, our small sense of self has dissolved. A complete vow is communicated directly to wisdom through this opening of the gates of the self.

A complete vow is heard. Wisdom answers and validates it. A complete vow is alchemy. It transforms your experience of body, energy, and mind. A complete vow is fulfilled without fail. You may backtrack a little, you may fall into temporary disgrace, but a complete vow pulls you toward wisdom inexorably. No complete vow can ever be entirely broken or abandoned.

A complete vow is surrender to your real situation. We tend to think of taking a vow as a moment in which we pull ourselves together, get tough, and buck up. However, a complete vow is as sweet and natural as water.

Ordinary promises have their place. But we all know that if a friend says they'll be over for dinner, something might get in the way—a delay or an unavoidable change in plans. We make allowances for this possibility. Maybe the friend will just forget or decide not to be friends with us anymore. Anything can happen, even when a promise has been made.

In spiritual traditions, many people conflate ordinary promises and vows. Most of us, when we say we are taking a vow, are only making an ordinary promise in fancy dress.

It is important to recognize that a spontaneous vow and a promise are different situations. A vow is not a grim affair. When we are committing to undertake some action, sometimes we sigh with tiredness at the thought of having to live up to our promise. But we experience a feeling of relaxation and joy when uttering a true vow.

We can never break the commitment to realize our own essential nature. This "natural commitment" is built into the life process itself. We can be ignorant of this, or we can consciously participate by doing sadhana, but either way, everything we do will express the desire to discover the nature of the Self.

Any true spiritual commitments and vows we make along the way—such as commitments to do practices or commitments to teachers through the process of initiation—are actually re-affirmations of the natural commitment to awakening that is born in the blood. This is why Anandamayi Ma said that if a commitment to a teacher can be broken, it never happened. It was just an ordinary promise from the start.[10]

Remembering and Forgetting

Sitting Down

Spiritual practitioners quickly learn that their unfoldment progresses in a pulse-like manner. We go through times during which all of our obscurations, confusions, and tensions come out to play. At other times, we are the embodiment of equanimity. Experiences of joy, confusion, doubt, clarity, gratitude, and upsetness with God move through us like waves that meet the shore and then recede back into the sea.

Spiritual practice is destructive. It destroys obscurations of our essence nature. It destroys what is temporarily blocking the full and natural flow of intelligence, compassion, skill, self-knowledge, and creativity. One way of describing these obscurations is as a forgetting of what we really are. Realization is recognizing and remembering.

Flashes of self-recognition come and go as we work with our teachers and practice. But by continually pausing to savor moments of greater relaxation and recognition, we get the "taste" of realization. We try our best to remember and remain in that condition. Many teachers have spoken eloquently about this as a process of stringing the moments of greater relaxation together like pearls until you have a whole necklace.

When we remember our essence nature, we feel ease, spaciousness, and delight. When we forget, we feel tense and alone. Through the pulse of coming and going during the course of sadhana, we eventually dance "backward" to rediscover the unconditioned Self.

Embody, Don't Embalm

One of the most useful pieces of advice about spiritual experiences I have received is this: Throw out everything and see what's left.

Seems like a simple statement, right? But when you investigate further, it's rather enigmatic. What does it mean to throw out everything? And what is left when you do so? Here's what I've learned.

First things you should throw out, of course, are those experiences you've made up, exaggerated, embellished over time, or elevated beyond reason. These include random shadows and flashes; hokey "coincidences"; candles "mysteriously" blowing out or similarly silly stuff; wishful thinking; vaguely spiritual dreams; contrived visions (You read it in a book and now it's happening to you!); and outright lies.

If you even suspect your "spiritual experience" falls into one or more of the categories above, be vigilant! Err on the side of caution, and toss it in the round file (the trash can). Stop talking about it, analyzing it, or attaching any importance to it.

Some of these kinds of events may relate to your practice or not. They may derive from realms other than human or not. They may be indications of past and future lives or not. Whatever. They are of little significance within the larger context of self-realization.

Real spiritual experiences always convey some actual wisdom. But instead of working to create the conditions that will turn a spiritual experience into a new basis for living, we often take that little experience into our psychic workshop and begin the lengthy embalming process.

We "fatten up" the experience with spiritual aura. Then we shape it into a coherent story. We graft on the super-spiritual meaning so everyone gets how special we are. Finally, we embed the entire apparatus into a block of ego plastic so we can carry it around and drag it out at spiritual gatherings.

By the time we're done, the wisdom is lost, and all we've got is another self-image formation. The opposite of wisdom.

When you are capable of opening to an authentic and significant spiritual transmission, whether it be from a live teacher, a dream, a vision, a flash of insight, or a life circumstance, you will notice that it is not available to your usual activities of making stories and analyzing. You can try lobbing some analysis at it, but your attempts will bounce away like rubber balls hitting a wall.

Authentic and significant spiritual transmission (wisdom experience) has a quality of imperviousness. You can feel it. When an experience can't be explained, believed, disbelieved, analyzed, narrated, or even thought about in your usual ways, there is something of value being transmitted.

Far from being fodder for an overactive self-image forming mechanism, real spiritual experiences are often rejected by the everyday mind. But "deeper" than this rationalism and drive for coherency is a shift in our form of life.

Real spiritual experiences transform our bodies, minds, and energy. They transform how we feel, what we know, and our capacity for kindness and equanimity. Real spiritual experiences reveal capacity and skill that was previously obscured by fixation and habit pattern. This is what is "left" when we throw out everything else.

Wisdom conveyed through spiritual experience is a live thing. It has its own intelligence and life process. It has real effects on our View and conduct. Our attempts to make the experience into a story or to understand it in conventional ways, generally kills our ability to make good use of the transmission.

So, if you've got some polished up spiritual experience story you've been lugging around, you can be sure it no longer contains the active principle. You've got the snake skin, but the snake got away.

Authentic spiritual experiences are not endings; they are beginnings. Spiritual experiences are work orders. You receive a "hit" of a more expanded way of being in the world. Now you have to do the work to stabilize that experience and integrate it into your life permanently. Embody, don't embalm.

Spiritual Opportunity

Everything that happens here in the manifest world is a communication that has the potential to help us to wake up and discover our real nature. When we notice one of these communications, we might call it a coincidence, an omen, synchronicity, or a special moment of grace.

But this alive, aware reality is made of wisdom, and its communications are continuous. We just don't always recognize it. Our karmic conditioning acts like a strange drug that keeps us from acknowledging or receiving what we are being offered.

While we are living in time, we are subject to cause and effect. Even if we are doing sadhana and are waking up, we lack total clarity. We are bound to miss some opportunities because our senses, including our minds, are still conditioned.

Imagine that a wonderful teacher announces a retreat. You feel an initial joyful impulse. Your heart responds with a spontaneous and immediate "yes!" Then conditioning sets in.

You are afraid to ask for time off at work. You are worried about money. Your friend or partner wants you to do something else at the time of the teaching, and you don't want to disappoint. You think the teaching is too far, too long, too late, or too early. Or you are tired. Or you are nervous about being with a new spiritual community. Infinite obstacles can arise. These are nothing more or less than failing to follow your own spontaneous wisdom. Your wisdom, which initially announced itself, has been obscured by karmic conditioning.

Karma is a real force. It is consciousness and energy repeating a pattern with momentum in time. Karmic patterns repeat without regard for the uniqueness of each moment. Whether pleasant or unpleasant, karmically bound activities always represent some kind of limitation.

In order to begin to release ourselves from karmic conditioning, we must achieve a certain level of clarity about our real situation. We must be able to recognize when we are being dragged off by karmic momentum.

Karmic momentum comes with a certain compulsive, anxious-feeling texture. Even if we are tumbling along in a pleasurable pattern, we can recognize this feeling of attachment. It is not so hard. Once you train yourself to recognize, you can begin to choose differently. That's the hard part!

Even if you can't see or feel clearly what is happening, you can take advantage of the insights of your teachers, friends, family, and fellow practitioners. Use everything at your disposal as a mirror.

Engaging in more appropriate movement in the face of karmic momentum is effortful. Yet it is the kind of effort that eventually frees us of karma so that we can experience kriya.

For instance, when you do daily spiritual practices, you are repurposing your body, energy, and mind to create a new *samskara*. A samskara is a karmic pattern, literally a mark or groove in reality. We are using our capacity for creating habit pattern to create new habit patterns that eventually free us from karma and introduce us to kriya.

Kriya is spontaneous, unbound activity. Kriya is activity that is perfectly in tune with nature and does not reinforce karma. Kriya is

81

Sitting Down

effortless and improvisational.

Kriya yoga is a system of sadhana that works with the natural flow of the subtle breath, or prana, in subtle channels and chakras. We learn to enter into and participate with the spontaneous movements of the subtle body. This helps us to move from karma, or bound activity, to experiencing true spontaneity.

We all pass up opportunities for growth. We don't do our practice with consistency. We miss teachings. Or perhaps we experience certain spiritual openings and then we don't do the work to make these our home base.

At a certain stage of sadhana, when I felt even the slightest tingle of awakening energy, I would stop what I was doing and would sit to do practice. Try to follow the impulse of wisdom when it says "yes!" to spiritual opportunity. When you feel an opening, take advantage and do some practice in that moment. Integrate your practice during your time off of the cushion. Reach out with your senses to people and circumstances and try to sense the subtle flows of communication continuously happening there.

Most of all, apply your practice. Don't compartmentalize life into "regular" and "spiritual." Bring your practice with you. Continually invoke the feeling of the fruit of your practice or of being with your teacher. Bring your life onto your path, and you will discover more opportunity to wake up and more grace than you ever knew existed.

Spiritual Growth

Am I experiencing real spiritual growth, or am I indulging in fantasy and wishful thinking? Every person doing spiritual practice should ask this question continually.

Spiritual awakening is the opposite of fantasy and trancing out. If you want to discover primordial awakeness and explore the fullness of human life, you must learn to recognize fantasy, and you must take steps to minimize opportunities to fall into fantasy.

Real spiritual growth is not a sensation or a vision. It is not a cool dream. Often, it's not even an initiation or empowerment. These phenomena sometimes open the door to spiritual growth or signal that growth is possible, but growth means one thing: a bigger View. You learn more about who you are and about reality, and you come to embody that. It is not a one-off experience.

Working with an experienced teacher who has some realization and can guide you based on first-hand knowledge is fundamental. My teachers have always asked me specific questions about the fruit of any practice I was doing, and they let me know when I was falling into wrong View, or fantasy. This is invaluable.

Some of my teachers have told me ahead of time about signs that a particular practice is developing correctly and bearing fruit. Reality speaks to us in precise languages about our various circumstances.

Here are three of the most important signs of real spiritual growth.

Real awakening always shows up in day-to-day conduct. You will relate to people and situations differently.

If you have gained the fruit of a practice, you will embody the fruit, not just have some concept or fleeting experience of it. It may take quite some time to be able to integrate the relaxation and expansion we gain from practice into our everyday lives, but this is ultimately what real spiritual growth is about.

Spiritual growth is about embodying usable wisdom.

When we experience real growth, we find we understand more about how reality works. We can participate more fully based on this understanding. Spiritual experiences that remain on the level of physical or emotional sensation are incomplete. They are good first steps, but we can know from this limitation that we still have a ways to go. Usable wisdom is the destination.

Spiritual growth has an impervious, vajra quality.

Real spiritual accomplishment is calm, self-luminous, and self-evident. It doesn't need any dressing up or supports. It doesn't need to announce itself other than by showing up.

Sitting Down

Suffering, Fear, and Pain

When I first came to spiritual practice, I didn't know I was suffering. I thought I was enjoying life and just looking for more. I had a lot to learn about myself and reality!

For instance, if you are enjoying your relationships, your job, your kids, your possessions, or anything else you have in your life right now, imagine that something is taken away. How will you feel?

If you are at a party, and someone you don't like arrives, do you feel tense? If your boss gets mad at you, do you freak out or lash back? If someone dies, do you grieve inconsolably? If you get sick, do you feel victimized and scared?

This is one way of looking at human suffering. At every moment, our so-called happiness is dependent on having or not having certain things and circumstances. We try very hard to hold onto the things we think will make us feel good, and we push away the things we don't like. We live in a near-constant state of defensive anxiety. Much of our life is spent trying to avoid recognizing our fear of life's openness. This is suffering.

Another source of suffering is that most people are experiencing compulsion most of the time. We have to do things and have things a certain way. We define ourselves very narrowly. We experience habitual emotions, activities, and reactions to life. We can't stop planning and thinking.

Once you get a little bit into a spiritual practice, you realize how much of a slave you are to your habits of body, emotion, and mind. This is what happened to me. I thought I was a free-wheeling kind of person. Then I began to notice all the ways of feeling, thinking, and acting over which I had surprisingly little control.

The root ignorance—our belief that we are separate individuals—is the basis for all suffering. We are firmly convinced that we are born as individuals and that we die. As a result, we feel cut off from our essential intimacy and continuity with all of existence. We are lonely, and we are afraid of death. Our habits and compulsions distract us from these difficult feelings.

Suffering happens when we are attached to habits of body, energy, and mind that distract or divert us from directly experiencing pain. Pain itself is not suffering; it is simply a certain quantity and quality of energy. We have to be willing to touch our pain directly if we are to live authentic lives and self-realize.

Our fear of pain and loss is very alive. Fear is an intense form of energy. When we run from our fear, we are running from our own vital energy. When we run from our loneliness, we are running from authentic understanding and the possibility of experiencing open-hearted compassion for ourselves and others.

As practitioners, we have to get fully and directly in touch with our condition of feeling separate and scared. The more we do this within the context of spiritual practice, the more we learn about ourselves and the more determined we become to discover our real nature.

Fear is an immensely alive state. Remember a moment when you felt really terrified. Electricity races everywhere in your body. Your skin seems to bubble and then disappear as you are launched into a field of energy and space. The conceptual mind short-circuits at the same time that the world appears to your senses with shocking clarity. The immediacy can be overwhelming.

Fear delivers us to boundless, unreasonable, uncontainable, nameless life. So we are actually afraid of fear because fear is a powerful and direct gateway to nonconceptual, supercharged openness.

My tradition, Trika Shaivism, is often associated with sexual acts. In fact, practices that invoke fear are much more common. In my life as a Tantrika, I have jumped off of high walls, been buried underground, and have meditated in woods where bobcats and other wild animals roamed.

I have learned that fear is a powerful ally. I have learned to bring fear onto my spiritual path. You can try to do this, too.

You need to begin by understanding that anxiety and fear are not the same. Worrying is what we do to avoid experiencing the piercing quality of fear. But if you have some circumstance in your life that gives rise to real fear—for instance, if you are afraid of flying in an airplane—you can use this to help you to realize.

The first thing you want to do when you feel fear is to consciously relax your body. This will cause the fear to race through you and will bring on a feeling of free fall. Then, you want to invoke a relatively formless, eyes-open meditation practice. A form of meditation that involves watching your thoughts or your breath will not work so well.

You can also chant a mantra. However, if you use a mantra in this situation, you cannot cling to it as a distraction. You are not trying to antidote the fear. This is the most important point.

Chant the mantra steadily and slowly with your eyes open. If the mantra is related to a Guru or Deity, you can have a real experience of that being, very large in space in front and slightly above you. But again, don't cling to a visualization. You have to allow yourself to relax into an actual experience of presence without any alteration of your condition. Keep relaxing your body.

You will feel the energy of the fear moving around within you. It

Sitting Down

will be uncomfortable, but interesting. Just let it keep unfolding. As you continue, you will learn much about your condition. If you keep on continuing, many wonderful openings can occur.

Spiritual Birth Pains

Various physical aches and pains can accompany the process of spiritual unfoldment. Some of the grosser manifestations of spiritual birth pains are: bands of painful tension across the forehead, uncomfortable sensations of pressure at the third eye or at other points on the head, spiritual "flus," stabbing pains, soreness at *marma* points (like acupuncture points), and exhaustion.

When we are practicing consistently, we are literally making ourselves available to a rebirthing process. This rebirth is not metaphorical. As a result of spiritual unfoldment, our form of embodiment; our body chemistry; our perceptions; and our way of moving, feeling, and sensing in the world will change.

If you are practicing an hour or more a day, at some point you will feel ill. Don't treat spiritual birth pains with painkillers. Just continue your sadhana. Adjust your diet and your level of effort so that your body has the nourishment it needs and the time to recalibrate.

Your entire system is undergoing a shift, and cultivating deep relaxation is usually the best way to participate. Try to remain quiet and relatively inactive so that you can relax deeply and allow the process to complete without too much interference.

If you are concerned about your symptoms, or if you are concerned about misinterpreting them and being in a state of fantasy, see a doctor. I knew a practitioner who thought he was becoming enlightened, but he was really suffering from heart disease. He waited too long to see a doctor and had a heart attack.

In the normal course of sadhana, nearly everyone experiences some physical discomfort related to sitting. A good way to orient yourself correctly to these events is to recognize how difficult it is for many people to sit in a meditation posture when they are just beginning. But one day, even a beginner might notice that all of the pains of sitting have simply disappeared. Then the next day, the pains are back. Eventually they go away for good. We know that this is not just a matter of the muscles stretching out, because the pain can disappear for periods of time even when a person is relatively new on the path.

Pain is a symptom of limitation in the physical body and the energy body simultaneously. These are differing expressions of the same body. In some moment, even a beginner may experience the relaxation of limitation. This comes and goes until relaxation stabilizes on more subtle levels. The truth is, we mostly become comfortable sitting in a meditation posture because we have relaxed from the inside out, not because we have stretched our muscles a lot.

For more aggressive, "heroic" practitioners, noticing their exhaustion can also be a signal that relaxation is occurring. Most people in contemporary society are chronically exhausted. But we push through this and mask the feeling of exhaustion with stimulants. The first spiritual experience that many people have is feeling how exhausted they really are.

When we are going through an opening, it is normal to experience a kind of seasickness. We are literally opening to wisdom, to embodied understanding. Our View is enlarging and the opening of the gates of perception can cause a temporary feeling of illness as when one is unaccustomed to travel on the open sea.

Sitting Down

I regularly experience changes in my sense of smell, hearing, and taste in response to spiritual growth. This makes sense because we are made of the five elements: earth, water, fire, air, and space. These elements are related to our senses. Doing a lot of sadhana causes shifts in how the elements show up in us. I know a shift is occurring because food starts to taste funny, or my sense of smell becomes more acute.

We come to spiritual practice with certain imbalances in our five elements. Our practice must be specifically tailored to address these imbalances and avoid causing harm to ourselves. A great deal of insight, experience, and discernment is necessary. For 99.9% of us, a teacher is absolutely required if we hope to progress and not fall into fantasy and unnecessary encounters with health imbalances.

Several well-known published accounts of the rise of kundalini have been written by people who were apparently quite unprepared for the experience. Unfortunately, the experiences recounted in these books have been taken for the norm. As a result, many people believe these extremely uncomfortable symptoms are desirable signs of spiritual growth. They are not. They are symptoms of blockage.

It is not out of the question that a person could die if gross disease is incorrectly attributed to spiritual practice or if practice is done incorrectly without proper guidance. During the course of my sadhana, I experienced some severe symptoms such as fever and heart irregularities. I am extremely grateful to my teachers for assisting me in these times, particularly for helping to have a correct View of such episodes. I needed to understand that my symptoms were the result of sick effort and were not badges of spiritual heroism or superiority. With the guidance of knowledgeable teachers, many of symptoms can be minimized or avoided altogether.

Practitioners sometimes become attached to uncomfortable symptoms or to any manifest physical sensations that arise during the course of practice. Remember that the fruit of practice is actual,

Sitting Down

usable wisdom, not just sensation. We will experience various sensations along the way as we deal with tensions and then relax. Some of these sensations are indicators of openings, but sensations are not the goal. Wisdom is the goal.

5.
Growing Up

Spiritual maturity means making a sincere effort to be in the state of your practice no matter what is happening.

Following

One night, Anandamayi Ma came to me in a dream and gave me an instruction that I didn't want to follow. I argued with her. She looked into my eyes and wagged her Guru finger at me. She said sternly: *You are shishya* (disciple). *I am Guru. Your only job is to obey instantly!*

Okay, I answered simply. *Okay*, she replied and smiled at me. My senses and awareness became suffused with bliss and clarity that lasted for days.

When we are just starting out on the path of sadhana, small I is in charge. Small I struggles, asks for help, prays, and does mantra and other practices, often in a state of desperation.

More importantly, small I plans, decides, and fights to maintain its false sense of independence. When that is threatened, small I throws tantrums and tries to bargain.

Life is happening. Only karmic habits cause us to take up particular stances toward this ongoingness. We commonly try to establish a sense of ground, personality, and boundaries by repeating positions such as: I like it or I don't like it, that it is good or bad, that is beautiful or ugly, or that is acceptable or unacceptable. We also categorize ourselves and others in order to create an experience of boundary and permanence.

Later, small I relaxes and spreads out a little bit, edging closer to discovering that it is a limited echo of the *Aham* or "I Am" of all of reality. When small I finally lets go, and becomes dissolved in the living presence of Aham, that is liberation.

When we are tense, we don't communicate well. But when we are more relaxed, we hear more and can respond more appropriately. When we are not so busy defending small I, we start to notice that the world is offering us guidance and assistance. We can stop struggling. We can stop declaring our independence. We can embark on the path of listening and following.

The moment when small I stops aggressively planning, deciding, and seeking is a milestone. You are understanding more and more that freedom doesn't mean that small I gets whatever it desires! That would be a terrible outcome, because whatever little I desires at this moment is shaped by extreme limitation. By following your teachers and the wisdom hints granted to you as you move through various circumstances, you can discover who you really are, not just who small I thinks you should be.

I follow my Guru, and I follow the wisdom that speaks to me through my heart, other people, dreams, omens, and circumstances. I follow divination, and I follow astrology. These are all modes via which wisdom guides me. I hardly ever make a decision. I hardly ever plan anything. I listen, and I respond.

I feel a lightness of being in living this way. I feel more playful and free of attachment. Even when wisdom instructs me to restrict myself in some way in order to play in the field of duality more skillfully, I feel incredibly grateful. The myriad ways in which wisdom cares for its creations are wonderous.

Following leads us away from attachment and toward greater freedom of self expression. You can express your nature in a spontaneous, natural, uncontrived way. You are not conditioned by past, present, and future. You are not conditioned by so much karma.

Your life feels more and more like improvisational music.

Many people cannot imagine a life of following. They have some idea that following is weak or dangerous. They cannot envision a life free from worrying about what will happen and free from trying to control life and manage fear.

Anandamayi Ma often repeated the Bengali phrase *jo ho jaye*. Jo ho jaye is usually translated as " whatever happens happens," or "wait for whatever happens." Jo ho jaye is not a statement of fatalism or nihilism. It is an instruction for yielding and taking refuge in life.

Try to relax your compulsion to accept, reject, categorize, fix, and manipulate everything. Use your practice to develop more sensitivity to what is actually unfolding and to respond and adapt to that. Learn to follow life's lead. For most of us, this happens little-by-little, step-by-step. Remembering jo ho jaye can support us in this process.

Inevitably, following brings deeper relaxation and more moments of simple, spontaneous, skillful responsiveness. By following and taking refuge in wisdom, a deep and abiding confidence in life begins to develop. You come to understand, in an embodied way, that the instruction, the giver of instruction, and the follower are one.

Growing Up

Adventuring in the Dark

When people begin a spiritual practice, they generally have some idea of what the fruits should be. They want to find peace, acquire special abilities, or become "enlightened" according to their concept of enlightenment. But any ideas you have of the fruits of practice are limited by your current condition. Most of what small I can imagine is dull, dry dust compared to the fruit of coming into contact with the blazing, aware aliveness of reality.

This is why it is always advised to practice without being attached to a preconceived goal. You should do your sadhana with the orientation of an adventurer or explorer. What will you find? Practice in a state of open perception, not with expectations.

Inevitably, practicing with concepts about practice leads to frustration, desperation, and feelings of failure. Small I starts to realize that its days are numbered, yet it keeps trying to get what it wants. Perhaps spiritual practice felt lovely in the beginning. Now it seems to not be "progressing." At times you feel afraid, or bored, or angry, or dried up. This isn't what you signed on for.

You become desperate, so desperate that you will even keep up your practice in spite of your "self." You just don't know what else to do. It seems that your spiritual life is falling apart. All of your former spiritual ego gratifications are being denied. You can't tell if you are slipping backwards or moving forward.

You feel that sadhana is your life raft, but you don't even know where you are headed. You have lost all sense of goal and direction. This is a good sign. Now is the time to just keep going, day-by-day, even in darkness. Great humility and confidence can be established at this point as wisdom carries you into deeper surrender.

Back in the 16th century, the Christian mystic St. John of the Cross wrote about the dark night of the soul. He captured for every age thereafter the essence of times during which spiritual seekers are inevitably confronted with the reality of their own attachments.

The first dark night of the soul generally occurs for sincere practitioners when the blush of initial enthusiasm for the spiritual path begins to give way to the recognition of the reality of our bondage to our compulsive patterns of body, energy, and mind. This is a time to sit quietly and allow obsolete self-concepts and spiritual concepts to fall away.

In contemplation in the space of the heart, we can discover the diamond-like natural longing that is our true inheritance, our royal road to wisdom. It is time to discover the indestructible wisdom that got us onto the path in the first place.

This initial dark night of the soul is also the time to cry out, to reach out, and to ask for nourishment from our teachers and communities. It is the time to bow our heads to our real circumstance and keep sitting even in the midst of frustration or despair. If the dark night of the soul is traversed with courage and patience, we can learn to have confidence in the loving responsiveness of life to our sincere efforts.

While this is a description of a possible experience you might have early in your life as a practitioner, we cross many such transitional "deserts" or dark nights if we practice throughout our entire lives. We eventually learn to recognize them as times when what needs to fall away is falling away. The new has not yet arrived. In between, the experience of lostness becomes a friend that we know is a harbinger of growth if we only agree to stop struggling and keep practicing.

Protect your practice

We all have limitations. Being blind to these, or trying to rise above them with applications of spiritual View that you have not yet embodied, will slow your unfoldment. No students and few teachers can digest every situation.

Sometimes we have to leave a circumstance in order to protect and support our practice. For instance, we may need to rearrange our work schedule or move to a more conducive environment. We may even have to end a relationship or a friendship or take some other fierce measure in order to protect our ability to continue our practice.

One time I was teaching a meditation seminar in California. A woman in the seminar told me that she lived in an apartment right next to a busy road. She found it difficult to meditate because of the constant noise. She asked me what she should do.

A young man dressed in spiritual-looking attire was listening in. His hands were positioned at his heart as if he were praying. He looked at me expectantly.

"Move!" I told her.

The young man looked visibly shocked.

"I thought you were going to tell her that she should be able to practice even with the noise! But you told her to give up and run away!" His tone of voice was a bit disapproving. I'm sure he now thinks I am not such a good teacher!

The longing to wake up and discover who you really are is the strongest and most enduring power in a human life. It is your birthright and the voice of God within you. Once this longing has caused you to recognize your real destination, head there as quickly as you can. Protect your practice. Don't let anything, not even pride, stand in your way.

6.
Taking the Long Way

There are many ways of getting stuck or waylaid on the path to waking up, but freedom is always victorious.

Karmic Entanglement

When we are doing any kind of spiritual practice, or just living our lives, we naturally want to move toward a condition of less tension, attachment, and emotional fixation. These are the symptoms and textures of karma.

Karma means limited activity. Karma is consciousness and energy repeating a pattern of limitation in time. In a relative sense, what creates limited activity is limited View.

For instance, a person has the View that they are second best and are always in danger of being passed over. This View engenders a habit pattern of vigilance and competitiveness. They are always trying to overcome their inner feeling of being second best by proving externally that they are better than everyone. This person gets stuck in this pattern until they learn more about their real nature.

The more that people with this style of karmic patterning keep fighting and struggling to prove themselves, the deeper and wider the entanglement will become. They will create new situations with other people who become involved with their tension. These situations will need to be resolved.

Most people cannot go through life without creating at least some further entanglement. This is the human condition. Most of us are not going to be able to resolve all of our karma in one lifetime. But we should understand that it takes time and energy to resolve karmic entanglements. Wouldn't it be better if we could use that time to do our practice and relax?

Those of us on a conscious path of waking up should try to minimize the degree to which we create more tension within ourselves and project that onto people and situations. If you reduce your level of entanglement, you will experience more clarity and energy in your practice and more freedom of expression in this life.

In all of our karmic fixations, there is always an element of pleasure. Pleasure is actually the root of attachment. We experience pleasure even as we are suffering. This is obvious when we are talking about a karmic pattern such as food, drug, or alcohol addiction. But it's also true about emotions we chronically generate such as frustration, anger, and jealousy.

It is fun to act out our frustration, to stomp around in anger, and to vent our jealousy. It is also pleasurable, on some level, to talk incessantly about our sorrows and problems.

Aside from the pleasure of running our energy through these emotions and activities, all karmic patterning is an attempt to resolve the root ignorance: our feeling of separation. We are trying to connect no matter how misguided our efforts may be.

The pleasure at the heart of fixation is some momentary experience of intimacy or connection. If we are violent toward others, we are still connecting. However, connecting by yelling at others does not get the result we most deeply want. When we lose our friends because we mistreated them, we are made even more aware of the pain of separation.

I call this "bad stop." We should have stopped going in the direction of entanglement and exhaustion long ago, but we ignored all the warning signs. Now we are forcibly stopped. Everything that happens is grace. Bad stop is fierce grace.

We all go through this exact same process in ten thousand different ways. If we go the route of acting out our limited View, we end up at some point feeling our separation more. This continues until we feel our loneliness and longing intensely. We bottom out. Then we finally get how necessary it is to make more successful efforts to connect. Eventually, we can begin to redirect our efforts toward discovering our real nature and our intimacy with everything.

The first step is to recognize your karmic habit patterns and to try to feel and listen for the loneliness and longing they express and engender. Try to feel deeply the divine longing at the heart of even your most limited habits of body, energy, and mind. When you connect with your longing in this way, you will also discover more compassion for yourself.

Having felt it, you then have to take responsibility for this longing. Determine within yourself that you will do your best not to drag yourself or others deeper into entanglement. Don't criticize, disparage, cheat, lie, steal, or get involved in situations that will tie up your energy in guilt, regret, argument, or litigation.

Use your practice day-by-day to relax, take nourishment, connect, and renew. Organize your life so that everything you do has the goal of protecting your practice. You have to functionally manage your energy and your level of entanglement in this way in order to experience greater peace, intimacy, and freedom in your life.

Knowledge is Bondage[11]

Attachment to conceptualizing, categorizing, capturing, and displaying knowledge undermines spiritual practice. I have met people who are so unwilling to be seen as beginners, to make a mistake, or to take the smallest leap into the unknown, they cannot even begin a spiritual practice. They are completely paralyzed by attachment to knowing.

Others demand to know exactly what they will get from sadhana before they start. Or, they come to a teacher having already decided what it is they want to know. They want to acquire certain practices or knowledge as if the teacher and the teachings were a supermarket from which to pick and choose. This happens among students of even the most accomplished teachers.

A more common phenomenon is that students feel unable to follow what are called "pointing out" instructions. These are key instructions for aspects of sadhana that can never be technically precise. Upon being given a transmission of pointing out instructions, the student must intuit what needs to be done.

The teacher uses certain phrases that suggest a method or a destination, but the student has to feel her way. People who are anxious about knowing precisely what to do, or who are over-reliant on intellect, often have trouble following pointing out instructions. In general, many people find themselves in a state of resistance to the simple, relaxed, open-ended exploration of which deeper sadhana consists.

Being in control of knowing and knowledge is the way that people manage their overwhelming fear of the boundlessness and wild abundance of reality. We stake out our tiny little claim in the vast universe. We put a fence around our limited understanding. Then we sit inside our "property" as if our lives depended on it.

Attachment to knowing more, to knowing specific techniques, to spiritual achievements, and winning approval for what we know will never lead to realization. These pleasures must be surrendered.

It is painful to stop feeding these sweets to yourself. But at some point, even the conceptual understandings given to you by your tradition to help you on your way must be given up. You will just be here, feeling everything and finding out for yourself.

Embodied Understanding vs. Borrowed Knowledge

Embodied understanding means that the fruit of your practice shows up in every area of your life: waking, sleeping, and dreaming. You feel, behave, eat, and play according to the fruit of your practice.

Embodied understanding emerges over time when you have had good View teachings and consistently do practices that engage your energy, your senses, and your mind. Embodied understanding comes out of your entire being, not just your mouth.

Students, and even teachers, often trade in borrowed knowledge. Borrowed knowledge is conceptual. You've read it in a book or you've heard it "around." You have not actually realized this understanding experientially for yourself. You have not integrated this knowledge into your life, but you profess it to others as if it were your own embodied knowledge. Borrowed knowledge can be delivered as helpful advice to fellow practitioners; as theories, opinions, pronouncements, or musings; or when taking up the mantle of the teacher or Guru.

Borrowed knowledge often hops a ride when someone has practiced something—asana, a mantra, or meditation—and professes to have realized much beyond what has actually been embodied.

This is more likely to happen when a person has not had thorough instruction. The tendency is to over-interpret some minor result.

Borrowed knowledge always serves an identity construct. We wave the banner of our borrowed knowledge to assuage our fears and insecurities and as a method of self-pleasuring. Sometimes people build entire spiritual careers on largely borrowed knowledge. Borrowed knowledge is a great hindrance to real spiritual growth.

Embodied knowledge can never be completely captured in a description. It is not information. It can only be arrived at by practice and transmitted by someone who has realized that knowledge. Embodied knowledge does not depend on books, theories, belief, faith, trust, or opinions. We can read about our traditions and receive View teachings that correctly orient us to our practice. But in the end, only by doing consistent sadhana do we come to consciously embody reality more fully.

My experience in the U.S. is that many people, in a kind of innocent way, cannot tell the difference between embodied understanding and borrowed knowledge. People are firmly entrenched in the concept that intellectual understanding is understanding. Thinking and knowing in an ordinary way actually becomes people's main experience in life. This blocks students from being able to reach out and into life and learn in a more direct way.

People have forgotten how to use their senses, body, and more subtle energy to learn. Minds are reduced to thinking machines. The capacity to use the mind properly as the sense organ of curiosity has atrophied.

The practices of direct realization traditions are powerful. Done over a long period of time, they will entirely remake you. When we rely on borrowed knowledge, we are basically admitting that we don't understand the practices or respect them. We are also robbing ourselves of the opportunity to actually find out.

Apprenticing yourself day-by-day to the process of unfoldment, you can come to live a life of total relaxation, creativity, spontaneity,

Taking the Long Way

compassion, and wonder. Your birthright is to embody all of the wisdom virtues of this alive, aware reality. Compared to this, borrowed knowledge is a dry twig blowing in the wind.

In order to grow, you must look deeply into what the Daoist tradition calls your "treasury of worms." You have to face up to your own fears and tensions in order to relax them. Attachment to borrowed knowledge delays this process.

Letting go of all the ways in which you build fortresses out of borrowed knowledge means being willing to make mistakes, lumber around, embrace your confusion, and most of all, encounter the openness of "I don't know."

Think of how a baby learns to walk. This is how you need to do your practice. Step-by-step, feeling your way, getting up when you fall, crying when you need to cry, and continuing on with both determination and delight. Practitioners need to learn how to reach into life with their entire beings. They must learn, and in some cases relearn, how to actually find out.

Letting go without the support of our concepts, beliefs, and convictions can feel scarily insecure. Openness scares us at the same time that we long for it. But the longing we feel is really our best friend. It is the voice of God cutting through our limitations. Our longing for "something" is precisely our embodied understanding. And it's calling out for us to stop talking so much, start practicing more, and relax into not knowing so embodied understanding can arise.

Spiritual Talk

Contrary to popular opinion, talk is not cheap. When we speak excessively and unnecessarily, we lose energy and become depleted. Most people can relate to this common experience.

While talk is not cheap, spiritual talk is the most expensive of all. Spiritual talk falls into two main categories: talking about our spiritual experiences and offering opinions about spiritual practice and View.

When we share a spiritual experience with all and sundry, we dissipate the energy we could be using to make that experience our new home base. Spiritual experiences are not the end of practice, they are the beginning. Spiritual experience is a transmission and a call to do the work to stabilize and embody a new level of understanding. In order to do this, we need to contain and concentrate our energy.

Nine times out of ten, when people talk about their spiritual experiences, they are bragging and soliciting the admiration of others. This bragging can sound humble and fool everyone. You can even fool yourself. But at the end of the day (the end of your life), you will be just as prideful, fear-driven, and anxiety-ridden as ever. And even if there was some authenticity in the experiences you blabbed about over and over again, the wisdom will have been lost.

This does not mean that spiritual experiences should never be mentioned by anyone. Teachers talk about their own experiences, or those of others, to assist students in various ways. But you'll notice that most teachers are sparing in this regard.

You should relate your experiences to your teacher. A good teacher will be able to tell you something about the significance of the phenomena that arise as a result of sadhana. A teacher can also tell you about the phenomena that arise as a result of fantasy! Telling our experiences to a qualified teacher is an important part of developing spiritual discrimination.

By far the most expensive form of spiritual talk is spiritual opinionism. In most spiritual communities, and certainly in on-line spiritual communities, many opinions about spiritual practice and View are offered freely and frequently. Generally, those offering spiritual opinions do so with great confidence, smoothness, and verve.

We live in a culture that values knowing and information. We are extremely well-trained in conceptual thinking and in giving ready answers. In fact, we are trained in school and by our parents to sound as if we are sure of ourselves even when we are not.

All of this training is at odds with the skills we need to enter into an authentic spiritual practice. Skills that help us to realize are uncompromising honesty, a high tolerance for uncertainty, an attitude of soft openness to life, tolerance of doubt, and the willingness to try new things and make mistakes.

Whether you are racing around gathering information from multiple sources or standing on the corner handing it out, you are not listening. While you are exercising your cultural skills of knowing, informing, and explicating; while you are considering the ten different bits of advice you got today, the supreme speech of cosmic wisdom is being outshouted.

In order to grow, we must learn to listen deeply and follow what we hear. Quiet, deep listening is key. It is much better to listen and follow than it is to talk and lead.

Upset with Guru?
Look in the Mirror!

Students often miss opportunities to realize by treating what arises in relationship with their teachers in an ordinary way. This most often manifests when students get upset with a teacher's behavior or attitudes and then expend a lot of energy analyzing and criticizing the teacher. The relationship with Guru is for only one thing: self-realization. What you should be doing is examining yourself in the mirror of the teacher.

A *melong* is a metal disk, polished to a mirror finish. Melong are living symbols of the natural process of teacher and student working together. The teacher serves as a mirror into which the student can look and see his true image reflected. By fearlessly gazing into the melong, over time, students can clarify and expand their View and release themselves from limitation and fixation.

If you are a student who has found a real teacher, you should try to see everything that transpires between you as arising for your benefit in the mirror of the open state of teacher. If the teacher does something that angers, humiliates, or annoys you, spending a lot of time analyzing the teacher's personality or behavior will cause you to miss an opportunity to relax and grow. You are only causing delay if you focus on "what the teacher did to me;" or how you think the teacher should have spoken to you; or what the teacher, in your opinion, should have done differently. The teacher is the melong, the mirror. The focus of your inquiry should always be what you see in the mirror and your own reactivity.

One time I told a student a story about myself and my former teacher. For some months, when I would come and go, he would never say hello or goodbye. Even if I traveled long distances to receive teachings, he did not take any special notice of my arrival or bother to mark my leaving.

"How rude!" my student immediately commented.

Not so. My teacher was reflecting attachments with which I needed to work. Only by causing me the pain of feeling those attachments more acutely could I notice them enough to work directly to relax them. He was also giving me a living View teaching: We live in total continuity. There is no coming and no going.

My teacher was inviting me to greater realization. If I had reacted in an ordinary way, as did my student, I would have lost the opportunity. My real job was to notice my own suffering and to work with that using the tools of sadhana.

Of course, my teacher was deliberately provoking my reactivity. This is the norm in direct realization lineages. Those who gravitate toward this way of working with the teacher generally *want* to be provoked so that they can see their own tensions clearly and relax them more quickly. For this reason, direct realization is said to be a fierce path.

But there were many things my teacher said did that were *not* deliberate and that provoked me and others. Most teachers are not highly or fully realized. They have their own tensions and blind spots.

Students, especially in the U.S., make the mistake of trying to separate out the "realized" from the "not realized" aspects of their

Taking the Long Way

teachers. Again, this is putting the emphasis on the wrong party. The emphasis should be on *your reactivity*, not on your teacher's.

Presumably, you are studying with a teacher so that you can realize. You are not there to police or improve the teacher. You are there to work with yourself in the crucible of the student-teacher relationship. Everything that happens is part of the alchemy of this relationship whose only purpose is to help *you* to wake up. This includes all aspects of the teacher's personality: love it, or hate it.

Even the occasionally harmful things a generally good teacher does can be useful for a dedicated student who is working with their own karmic patterns. This does not mean everyone should remain with any teacher no matter what the circumstance. Of course you want to develop enough clarity so that you can avoid, or learn from and then leave, teachers who cause great harm to students. It *does* mean that if you have decided to work with a teacher, you will get the best result for you if you treat the entire circumstance as the teaching.

While some students fall into ordinary habits of teacher analysis and critique, other students fall into stupid adulation. They want the teacher to validate their choice of a teacher and serve as a kind of spiritual accessory. Or they just want to be saved, and so they need the teacher to be a savior. They interpret everything the teacher says and does as spiritually extraordinary. These students have no clarity and will most likely end up being upset once they notice their teacher's humanity.

Stickiness on the Spiritual Path

Someone once said to me: *I don't know how you've done it, but somehow you've managed not to get stuck in all the ways that spiritual aspirants usually get stuck.*

This is no mystery. I've had teachers prying me loose at every sticky turn.

Stickiness is attachment to people, relationships, experiences, and concepts, especially self-concept. All attachment is an attempt by small self to keep itself stuck together in a more or less static form. It all adds up to one big sticky, spiritual gumball.

I came into this world with attachments and developed new ones along the way. Many of our attachments are obvious. Some are very subtle. Treading the spiritual path can be like spending years trapped in a fun house. If you are practicing well, all of the attachments you never knew you had will pop out, do a scary dance, and laugh a scary laugh.

A special category of stickiness is attachment to spiritual concepts, projections, and experiences. How about that special spiritual dream you had three months ago that you are still talking about? Or the special spiritual voice you talk in to let everyone know you are spiritual? Or the fizzy sensation you once had that you worked up into a "kundalini" experience. And now you refer to it as "my samadhi?"

These are gross forms of spiritual fixation. These are obvious ways that small I condenses around spiritual stuff. Same old small-ness, just glossier stories. This sort of indulgence will not free you.

But all spiritual practitioners, even sincere ones, can easily get stuck. We get stuck because we are not taught proper View. We get stuck because we don't have a large enough perspective on reality to guide us past our fixations. We absolutely need View, and imparting View to a student is the most important job of any teacher.

People are naturally drawn to realizing their own nature. Your desire to wake up is an aspect of the energy that drives the entire life process. You learn to detach from what is sticking you to limitation, and you attach to that which will help you to wake up. Your sticky attachments are limited expressions of the same more generalized, expansive capacity to attach to that which guides you to self-realization. This is how our intelligent, alive reality works.

Attaching to our teachers, the teachings, and spiritual community is the leap that we make when we are moving to a less contracted, self-limiting state of attachment. The world in its infinite grace gives us these manifest guides to attach to so that we can discover primordial awakeness, which is ultimately groundless.

Guilt and Regret

Many people suffer from a tension they call "guilt." Guilt is a tricky little small I survival pattern. Guilt uses the mask of responsibility to avoid responsibility and maintain destructive habit patterns.

Guilt draws attention away from the reality of my actions and toward small self's feeling of guilt. By feeling really guilty, I try to fool everyone into thinking I am taking responsibility, but I am actually running away from responsibility and sucking energy out of others.

Usually, guilt demands sympathy from those very others who have been most affected by my action or inaction. Guilt is "me" focused instead of Real Situation focused. Guilt is a technique for evading responsible action.

If we injure an animal with our car, we try to do something to alleviate the animal's suffering. We don't stand idly at the curb moaning about how guilty we feel about the plight of animals. We don't demand that others attend to our guilt while leaving the actual animal to suffer alone. Or maybe we do.

Guilt always tries to perpetuate itself. Have you ever tried to talk a person out of feeling guilty? Guilt just uses this attention to fuel itself. No matter how sensible and reality-based you are with a guilty person, they can always return to the status quo by claiming I feel so guilty! In this way, cultivating guilt helps to keep the guilty person primed and ready to return to the same irresponsible behaviors.

How does this work? Guilt is a pay out. You do something destructive to yourself and others. Then you pay for your behavior with the "punishment" of feeling guilty. After this, you are free to return to the same pattern. Or likely you are in the pattern and feel guilty all at the same time. You pay as you go.

Guilty people also apologize without any real intention of changing their situation. Even worse is when they ask for forgiveness. Instead of quietly and efficiently rectifying their behavior, they ask someone else to perform the work of a priest.

For people who are stuck with guilt, this pattern usually happens over and over again. It's really exhausting. The guilty should get angry at guilt and its ploys. Guilt is like a bad houseguest who eats your food and leaves you with an enormous utility bill.

The truth is, none of us needs to be forgiven for our ignorance and mistakes. Having an experience of limitation is just a natural aspect of the life process. But waking up is being responsive and responsible to your real situation. You have the opportunity to practice and discover more of your human situation and its potentials, and you seize this opportunity.

A friend told me he felt guilty about something. Then he said, *I suppose Tantrikas don't feel guilty.*

True. But we do feel healthy regret. When we regret our actions, we are saying that we see their consequences, and we intend to do our best to relax the tensions that caused us to act in a certain ignorant way.

Regret acknowledges that we cannot change what has already happened, but we can have an impact on what is going to happen. This is responsibility without narcissism. Regret acknowledges the harm we have caused to ourselves and others, but it doesn't wring pity out of people.

No matter how destructive a pattern has been, we can always make a decision to use our practice and begin to relax those tensions. We can do better the next time. Sometimes we take vows to help us with this. Sometimes we are able, because of the grace inherent in the totality of a situation, to develop more clarity and change our patterning in that moment.

For people who habitually express their suffering in the form of guilt, to recognize the real nature of guilt can be an experience like taking a big breath of fresh, cold mountain air. Relaxing the grip of guilt to let in honest regret also lets in self-compassion and compassion for others. We are no longer locked up in our cage of guilt, continually reinforcing our root sense of separation. We can rejoin the human family, and even appreciate that clever trickster guilt as we say goodbye.

Life Sucks

If you have ever gone swimming in a fast-moving river, you know that you have to be a good observer of state of the river in order to know how to move in keeping with the shifting waters. You have to observe the many currents and rocks and other beings. You need good judgment and timing in order to stay afloat and on course. This is exactly parallel to our human lives.

Let's say we are doing a good job of balancing on a rock in the middle of the river of life. We are congratulating ourselves because we have managed not to be swept away. Our entire focus is on that rock. This is how many of us live. We try to keep everything static and safe-feeling while life roars around us.

Because our focus is so narrow and fixed, we do not see the crocodile coming. Standing so still in the middle of the river, we are perfectly placed to become a meal for the crocodile. All of a sudden—we are dinner!

How did that happen, you wonder from inside the croc's belly! I had everything together, perfectly balanced, and now Life Sucks!

The answer is bad timing brought on by ignorance, a.k.a. narrow View.

In order to act more fluidly and with better timing, we have to encompass a wider View. This is what spiritual practice is for—enlarging our View so that we can embody more spaciousness and presence and avoid being tumbled about by karma, good or bad. When we do practices such as mantra and meditation, our subtle channels and vision open. We come to embody more wisdom from the inside out.

When we embody a larger View, our senses become more precise and expansive. Our thinking has more clarity. We experience less confusion because some of our karmic entanglement has cleared. We are no longer so driven by anxiety or burdened with lethargy. We are free to move and adapt more skillfully.

Of course, most people on the planet are not self-realized. So we all have more or less bad timing. This is the human condition. What can we do?

First, when you hit a hard patch in life, pull yourself out of the misapprehension that you have been victimized or that life is unfair. Life is naturally uneven. You are not being punished for bad timing. You are human, and human life has its ups and downs. Bad timing is unavoidable. It is not a sin. It is a natural part of the life process.

On another level, everything that happens "to" you is a response, at least in part, to your activity, and it is a compassionate response. We are always being communicated to in every circumstance in a way that has the possibility to help us to wake up.

Don't spend a lot of time trying to figure out how you got yourself into a mess. It's good to reflect on missed signals and the moments in which you ignored your own wisdom. But having done so, move on. Turn your attention to the present. Try to discern the wisdom in your situation. Adapt to your new circumstances and work as skillfully with these as you can.

The river is flowing. A new situation arises in every moment. Being attached to explaining the past is just like clinging to a rock in the river. Eventually, every rock will become sand. So why not let go now and learn to swim?

No matter what happens, you are responsible for how you react to circumstance. Think of people who have been through very painful experiences such as incarceration, torture, rape, war, and serious illness. Some people make use of these experiences to grow. Others become traumatized by anger and fear. Still others, although very few, have done enough spiritual practice that they remain, relaxing in their own nature no matter what is happening.

The message here is that your reaction to life's circumstances is your reaction shaped by your karma. No one is causing you to react in any particular way.

Although we are responsible for our lives, we do have help. We can consult experts, our teachers, a good astrologer, or use a form of divination to help us to better surf the currents.

Our aim in consulting a Guru, astrologer, or diviner should be to discern the potentials in the present so that we can take responsibility for our life and use better timing to help make the best of what is to come. It should not be to figure out how we can be saved by predictions. This is unreal, and it is not responsible. Hard times inevitably come around. Just try to relate to them in a simple, practical way using the tools you have ready-to-hand.

Although it may seem counter-intuitive to some, when life is difficult, when you seem to have lost everything, that is the best time to offer service to your teacher, community, and anyone else who needs it. No matter what your circumstance, you can always be of service, even if it is just by offering a loving gesture to your fellow inmates!

Service helps us to reconnect with our real refuge in the divine Self and to rediscover natural nourishment and devotion. It teaches us that we always have something to give, no matter how much we have lost. We are always good and complete.

Star Trek vs. the Kali Yuga

Taking the Long Way

I grew up watching Star Trek with my mom. Somehow, rationalism, technology, and the scientific View have failed to deliver that shiny, clean world of unlimited exploration in which human beings get to lecture less evolved races on other planets about their bad behavior.

Instead, the individualistic greed of our human cultures has injured, not only the space program, but our air, water, land, and the lives of millions upon millions of people and animals.

Welcome to the *Kali Yuga*. The Kali Yuga is the final and darkest cycle of four epochs that make up the entire wheel of samsaric, linear time. "Darkness" means ignorance. Ignorance is ignorance of one thing only: your real nature. Each of the yugas is characterized by greater or lesser ignorance, by greater or lesser ability to do sustained sadhana, by easier or harder access to communication between subtle wisdom beings, humans, animals, and other realm beings.

The *Satya Yuga*, is the age during which people are closest to self-realization and therefore have the fewest karmic entanglements with which to contend. Following each Satya Yuga, human beings again descend along the wheel into greater and greater ignorance with each passing epoch.

People of each of the yugas benefit most from methods that best address their particular capacities. As the story goes, the appropriate sadhana for most people of the Kali Yuga is mantra japa and kirtan. In the Satya Yuga, more people are capable of engaging in subtle meditation and complex practices.

My experience is that the yugas exist both as a wheel of progressive epochs and simultaneously as possibilities for self-expression in *any* age. There is an overarching cyclical progression. This is like the path on a game board. At the same time, individual players (different beings) existing at the same point in linear time on the game board might be experiencing and be expressive of any one of the yugas.

Whether or not you have a concrete experience of the yugas, the progression of the four epochs expresses the understanding that reality has the capacity to beget ignorance and that the deepest ignorance still contains within it the seeds of realization. Hence, at the end of the final epoch, the Kali Yuga, the cycle begins again with a renewal of the Satya Yuga.

You can see this principle at work today. The extreme violence perpetrated against the nation of Tibet and its people has resulted in Tibetan Buddhism spreading all over the world. Before the invasion of Tibet, not a single lama was teaching outside of that small, inaccessible country. Now many more people have the opportunity to receive and practice authentic wisdom teachings.

This is, of course, a complex situation. People inside Tibet and those living in the diaspora are still suffering greatly, as are Chinese people, both those who have perpetrated violence and ordinary people. The denial of freedom on an ordinary level is the gross expression of the experience of separation.

The root ignorance is our conviction that reality is constituted of distinct entities or objects. Everyone suffers from the embodied View that we are separate beings. This conviction characterizes science, much of philosophy, psychology, and contemporary social life.

Physicists search for the basic "particle" of life. Doctors search for the causes of disease in individual genes. We wantonly kill other living beings and destroy our planet because we are cut off from empathy and compassion. It is difficult for most people to think beyond the question of "How does this affect me?"

Modern cultures are driven by the View that we can use mechanistic, scientific means to compensate for the losses in our environment and the toxins eating away at our blood, brains, and organs. As we kill off our bodies and minds, we fantasize about being saved by shiny new parts, impervious to death. Our scientists try to fix, for billions of dollars, what the simple recognition of interdependence and a little everyday compassionate sharing could set right for free.

Luckily for us, in the Kali Yuga, a small, steady, sincere effort to self-realize goes a long way. This is grace at work in our age. Look around you. You can easily see that discovering teachings is a marvelous opportunity. Take full advantage of this circumstance, but don't cultivate any heroic or superior "spiritual" attitudes. We in the West have done that for a long time. Spiritual lineages have cultivated competitiveness. The time when such attitudes can be indulged without recognizing the cruelty that they perpetuate has come to an end.

In an age of ignorance, it is best to cultivate gratitude rather than feelings of superiority. It is better to share the fruits of your practice by living alongside those who are mired in ignorance than to build walls—real walls or attitudinal walls. It is walls that got us here.

There is nothing to struggle against. The world takes care of itself. But we are this world, and we have our parts to play. Cultivating your practice so that you are able to express sincere kindness, empathy, and compassion is the way to go. If you are able to do this, give thanks. Give great thanks.

Taking the Long Way

Detours

One day, I got a speeding ticket. It just so happened that I was engaged in pushing ahead with plans that were not in sync with wisdom. I was being willful rather than responsive to life.

I remarked to someone that getting a speeding ticket and being told by Guru to slow down are exactly the same: a meaningful communication from reality. This person replied that perhaps I was just driving too fast. This is the kind of View that causes people to miss important communications from wisdom over and over again.

There is only continuity. Absolutely everything that arises is a response of Self to Self. Every accomplished practitioner arrives at this insight sooner or later. If you look, listen, taste, touch, smell, and reflect fully, you get to join the total conversation. If your senses and mind are limited, you miss aspects of the conversation entirely or respond inappropriately.

Wisdom, a.k.a. reality, is always trying to communicate with us. The purpose of the communication is to get us to become more aware and to self-recognize. If we don't listen to wisdom, we get another chance and another and another. Each opportunity grows more insistent like progressively harder knocks on the head. If we still don't listen, then whatever we were clinging to is usually ripped away. This is grace, even though it is painful.

On the other hand, sometimes our insistence is so high, wisdom responds by offering us a "detour." Detours work in one of two ways. Either we get what small I wants in order to satisfy a karmic pattern, or we exercise a karma until there is a breakdown. A detour might bring us resolution through fulfillment, or it might temporarily satisfy and then bring us to the point of becoming sick, poor, horribly lonely, or subject to some other kind of crisis.

Perhaps a particular person has the karma of never having fallen in love. To some other person, this might be unimportant, but to this person, the desire to fall in love dominates their life. Receiving that experience and feeling satisfied might allow the person to relax and move on.

Another person might have the karma of overeating. This person gets lots of opportunities to make a decision to adjust their lifestyle, but they are not ready. The compulsion is too strong. The detour involves becoming very sick. Eventually, the desire to overeat will be overpowered by the desire to live.

Detours are the long way around. Sometimes they last for only a few moments. In other cases, they last for lifetimes. But in general, a detour is resolving karma by living through it until it runs out of energy.

The shorter way is to use our inherent freedom to form new habits now that take us in the direction of natural relaxation and realization. We can also occasionally act so decisively to cut through an entangled situation that karma is over in an instant.

Infinite circumstances conspire to determine which path we can take in any particular instance. But eventually everyone must choose to cut through karmas, work to relax them, or go the entire distance until they die of exhaustion. It's just a matter of how long it will take and how much pain you will experience on the way.

If an opportunity to relax your tensions arises, you can be sure that if you say yes, you will succeed. But you can also say no for a

Taking the Long Way

while and extend your suffering. You may think you are choosing greater comfort, but that comfort is exceedingly temporary. You are just padding your prison cell. At some point, you will have to come out and play in the openness of life.

One night, I dreamt of a house. I was leading students outside into a vast, rolling landscape of shimmering color.

I said to them: How beautiful! How infinitely nuanced! How luminous! Please, please come.

Some stepped directly from the confines of the familiar house into the outdoors. Others were afraid and hung back. I wanted to wait for everyone.

When students meet the right teachings for them, a vast, subtle landscape opens out. Longing to explore that arises. There is recognition and a feeling of discovering one's true, unconfined home. This is a gap in karma, a gap in time.

But often, immediately following this gap experience, fear rushes in. Each person's fear of waking up takes a familiar karmic form.

What if I change too much and lose friends?

What if my spiritual practice interferes with my career?

What if my family freaks out?

I don't want to lose anything; I only want to add things.

I don't like to be in a group.

I don't like to feel uncomfortable; I only want to feel happy.

I don't like being asked to pay for teachings.

I don't need a teacher.

Teacher is not behaving as I want.

I want spiritual practice to be X, but the teacher wants me to do Y.

I'm confused.

I'm not capable.

This isn't the right time.

I'm too busy.

I don't want to travel for teachings.

I'm angry.

I just want to know how to fix my problems.

I have to understand everything thoroughly before I get started.

The culture of these teachings is strange to me.

I need the teacher, or my practice, to be miraculous. Nothing else will convince me to continue.

My teacher, Anandamayi Ma, manifested infinite patience. At the same time, she did everything possible to help people to recognize their real natures. She waited for students to be able to practice, and she tried to give them everything they needed to make that happen quickly.

If you want to release your resistance and self-realize a little more quickly, you must put yourself in situations that remind you of who you are, of your true home. You must make an effort to overcome the karmic momentum that takes the form of stories about why you can't, don't want to, or shouldn't do this.

Read the works of teachers you admire and biographies and autobiographies of practitioners. Attend teachings whenever possible. If you have a teacher, seize every opportunity to receive teachings from that person. If you have been given a practice, do it with consistency and constancy as if your life depends on it—because it does.

Try to remember that, although most of us will lead an ordinary life with ordinary responsibilities, the purpose of this entire manifestation is self-realization. Anything that you claim is standing in your way, no matter how reasonable-sounding, is only karmic vision. There is no reasonable reason not to step out of your limitations, other than the workings of limitation itself.

Time and karma are intimately related. Ma knew that everything has its time and also that it is possible to step out of linear time. So, on the one hand, it is perfectly fine that students take a long time to dedicate themselves consciously to self-realization. Every reason students give not to practice, every little bit of resistance, is just the life process itself unfolding in time.

131

Taking the Long Way

But if we can recognize the transmission of self-realization coming through our teachers, and if we can work to experience that in every moment, we have the opportunity to sidestep the full impact of our karma. We have the possibility to enter directly into the unconditioned, eternal moment.

7.
Being
Together

A spiritual community is a gateway to realizing your continuity with all beings.

Community is Sadhana

Direct realization traditions such as Tantra and Dzogchen have been householder traditions since their inception. We do not make an existential or moral distinction between spiritual and secular life. Self-realization means seeing the equality of all phenomena. No special form of life is required. Nothing needs to be artificially renounced.

Direct realization practitioners and teachers work, play, and have friends and families. We live among other householders. We don't wear renunciate robes or build ashrams. We are not generally sitting on mountaintops or hanging around in caves for long periods of time.

Starting in the 20th century, some lineages from both India and Tibet have practiced a synthesis of direct realization and other traditions. They have promoted ashrams and monasteries and standard, external forms of renunciation such as celibacy. But this is not the thorough direct realization way.

We look for the fruit of our practice, in part, in how we show up in everyday life. Our relationships with others are mirrors that reflect our real condition and are a vital aspect of our sadhana.

While we don't build ashrams, we have the understanding that it is extremely useful to participate in a spiritual community.

Mandala means a unified, territory, generally circular and three-dimensional. In direct realization traditions, mandala can indicate the larger group of people associated with a teacher or tradition. Mandala includes those following the practice closely, those who might come regularly only for satsang, and those who only occasionally attend a teaching. A similar word, *sangha*, is generally used in Buddhist communities to indicate a loosely-knit body of students.

Kula means "family." In Trika Shaivism, kula has always indicated those who have received *diksha* (formal initiation) and who live either with or very near to their Guru. Today, kula can mean those for whom a particular teacher and tradition are recognized as their spiritual home. It represents a deep commitment to practice and to organizing one's life around the axis of waking up.

The idea is not to position the teacher and a group of students as an exclusive spiritual club. When we become more realized, we will experience *all* of manifest life as kula, as the infinite family within the single body of the Supreme Shakti. The Guru Kula is training for this more all-encompassing experience of family.

Spiritual community members share important values and a consciously chosen direction. Because they have received teachings together, they share a common language. They can speak to each other freely about deep feelings that are often harder to articulate with other people.

Most importantly, working together with the teacher, community members develop capacities for openness, kindness, and honesty. Spiritual community is a gateway to expressing these wisdom virtues everywhere.

When we are participating in a spiritual community, we are intimately relating to diverse people. Students are often thrown together for long periods of time and are engaged in intense activities together. But the other students of the teacher are not friends

135

Being Together

that we choose for ourselves. For this reason, we will surely discover that we don't like some of the other students. We will find some of them difficult to get along with. This is very useful.

It is easier to fool ourselves about our degree of realization when we are just doing seated practice on our own and then relating only to those people who we personally choose. Sometimes in this situation, it is our relations with our birth families that can show us where the karmic tensions are hiding!

The goal of self-realization is not to love and care for a handful of people. Accomplished beings feel compassion and concern for everyone. This is our goal. The process of working within community helps us to open to a wider field of relationships.

If we are really doing the practice, and if we understand the View, we are more committed to relaxing our tensions and our expectations of others. We understand that the spiritual community is a training ground. Perhaps we entered the community with strong preferences for a few people. Eventually, we come to see the good in everyone in our community. This sphere of intimacy enlarges naturally if we just keep practicing. Eventually, it includes all beings and worlds.

A functioning spiritual community is not just a collection of individuals. The teacher and lineage masters are the central channel of the community. The students become part of the energy body of the lineage. Wisdom comes through the central channel for the benefit of everyone.

When the teacher does not hold the teachings and embody them with integrity, the body of the kula falls apart energetically and physically. The community becomes more of a parody, going through the motions and eventually disintegrating. Students should not be too concerned with this, as upsetting as it might be if you find yourself in such a community. Just pull up your stakes and move on. Nothing is ever lost if you are using everything that happens to help you self-realize.

Direct realization teachers use communities in special ways to help students realize more quickly. You may find yourself constantly thrown in with someone who rubs you the wrong way or continually pushed into situations that trigger your tensions. Plans may keep changing just when you thought you knew what was going on. You will find yourself to be both deeply challenged and relaxing to a degree you could not previously imagine.

As a kula member, your job is to remember the View and work to embody it in every situation. This does not mean that you try to act compassionately when you are really feeling crabby and selfish. It *does* mean that you try not to draw your spiritual family into your karmic drama.

Many of the practices people receive in direct realization traditions are integrated. This means that you do them in the course of life, not on a cushion, or not only on a cushion. Taking responsibility for your reactivity within the context of community means remembering your larger purpose and invoking your practice right in the middle of your reactivity. If you do this over and over again, eventually the wisdom virtues of kindness and compassion arise naturally. You do not have to manufacture anything; you just have to apply your practice and relax.

Being Together

The Lowdown on Lineages

Lineages are most often defined as successive generations of teachers who hold and can transmit particular streams of teachings. This is one manifestation of lineage, but it is not the whole story.

Lineages are like rivers. Each river has a different character that meets the terrain and supports the ecosystems depending on it, yet all rivers are composed of nourishing water. Just so, lineages are rivers of wisdom energy flowing from the Supreme Self to teachers and on to students through time. Each lineage meets the unique needs of those who are bathing in its waters, and yet all true lineage in some way supports the realization of continuity and the one taste of the creation.

Like the sustaining waters of Ma Ganga coursing down Shiva's locks of hair to moisten the parched land and slake the thirst of all beings, lineage is a supreme blessing. Those who sense her life, compassion, and immense intelligence are eager to dive in.

Sometimes lineages flow through vast expanses of time, powerful and unbroken. Sometimes they manifest seemingly with no precedent as eternal teachings arrive in the human realm for an altered age. Sometimes lineages hang on, having lost the capacity to transmit the wisdoms they once held. All manifest forms of lineage eventually resolve back to the unmanifest as new forms arise.

In order to be a teacher of the river, one must be a disciple of the river. This is the qualification. There is no real transmission without lineage, without the *abhisheka,* or blessing bath of the wisdom of the Mother. All lineages are Her. All transmission teaching flows as a response to discipleship to Her.

Sometimes the transmission of lineage explodes. At other times it appears as a piercingly clear gem emerging from mist. Mostly, the flow of wisdom is as a river: stately, implacable, yet playfully moving on, depositing understanding that is immediate and beyond any question of certainty or doubt.

I am not talking about a concept or some transcendental subtlety. The reception of wisdom energy is palpable, tangible, and even shocking or painful at times. You don't think it up, make it up, premeditate it or analyze it. It arrives through the medium of a human teacher, other beings, and circumstance.

> *There is but one Guru, the uninterrupted transmission of the rays (of awakened consciousness) passed on to us through the initiatory lineage.*

—*The Kaula Sutras*[12]

The Guru-disciple process is what the Supreme Self has given us so that we can learn to surrender and discover natural devotion. Discipleship is the finest flower of natural devotion. Even the Guru bows to a true disciple.

When we discover natural devotion, we realize the devotion of the scent to the nose, the taste to the tongue, the touch to the body of the world. We discover that the entire world is *puja* or ritual worship. We can experience and understand directly that a lineage of teachings is the most exquisite devotional offering.

Teachers who take the seat of spiritual guide when they have no real experience of discipleship are perpetuating their own karma and the suffering of others. To assume the role of a spiritual guide

Being Together

when one has only begun to swim in the shoreline eddies and flows of the river of devotion is risky because one might never leave that spot, or one might mistake the shoreline tide pools for the whole river.

Students sometimes devote themselves to teachers in order to make themselves feel safer or more important. Sincere teachers who do not yet have a real experience of discipleship can allow themselves to be lulled into fantasy by the fantasies of their students. Or they will even encourage these fantasies.

Committed discipleship to a teacher, to your own realization, and to a lineage of teachings sooner or later strips you of fantasy. Over time, you will gain a good sense of how to work with your limitations, and so you will have something of value to offer others.

A sincere teacher who practices discipleship before all else has the opportunity to serve students well. Most teachers are not fully realized, but if they become great disciples, the river will flow.

Spiritual Untouchables

Spiritual communities are famous for clannishness and infighting and for harshly ex-communicating those who trouble other members of the group. In some instances, it is teachers who set the tone for this kind of activity. In other cases, the teacher is not around, and the fixations of the students are free to mask themselves with egoic misapplications of the teachings.

A certain highly accomplished Guru traveled for the first time to a city where some students had formed a small group. Now, it so happened that, in the absence of Guru, one fellow had assumed the "top dog" leadership position in this group. He fancied himself quite an advanced practitioner, capable of giving teachings to students even though he had no permission from the Guru.

This fellow was quite attached to the enjoyment he derived from this role-playing. Far from being capable of leadership or of conveying teachings to others, his display of confidence and knowledge was totally contrived. Nonetheless, others were impressed and followed along.

So there this fellow was, playing the role of preceptor, when the real Guru showed up. The faux Guru didn't like the idea of being shut down. So he went into overdrive. He locked the real teacher out of the teaching hall.

It was evening and wintertime. The Guru was standing in the street. But he was resourceful and luckily did not freeze to death! The next day, the Guru called a meeting. To everyone's surprise, he extended a kind invitation to the student who had locked him out the previous evening. During that meeting, the clear seeing and compassion of the teacher acted like a reverse poison—a remedy. The student was freed of being possessed by his compulsion.

Under the gaze of the real teacher, the situation of the student could manifest more honestly. He was terribly afraid that others might find out how unworthy he felt. He longed with the grief of a little abandoned child for the Guru's love. But he felt so cut off from true love, he had tried to manipulate others into looking up to him and even fearing him.

The spiritual literature of India, Tibet, and many other places is filled with stories of accomplished teachers who encounter thieves, rapists, those possessed by greed, and even demons. With great insight and compassion, these teachers free other beings from fixation so that they can continue on the path to self-realization.

Students, all students, come to spiritual communities and teachers with their fixations, compulsions, and attachments on full display. The student who is obviously disruptive is no more troublesome than a student who tries to win the favor of the teacher with acts of false devotion and obedience or one who uses "the teachings" as a weapon against other students.

The greatest teachers neither seek nor reject students. All are welcome. However, this does not apply to every teacher. It only applies to those teachers who can truly be of benefit to the incredibly diverse beings they meet. The rest of us have to know our limitations and how these determine whom we can benefit and whom we cannot.

If a student is unteachable by a certain teacher, this is a reflection of the limitation of the teacher. So-called "bad" students should never be vilified by teachers or communities. We are all "bad" students until we are self-realized. It is only a matter of degree.

This world, composed of nothing but intelligence and compassion, teaches everyone without exception. This is cosmic law. No one is unteachable. Only individuated teachers with their own limitations are not yet fit to serve everyone who comes their way.

Here are three golden rules for working with difficult situations within spiritual communities.

Treat any reaction you have to another person or situation as your responsibility.

Your fixations are your karma; they are what you have to take responsibility for and work with. They are not caused by anyone else.

The member of your community who irritates you is, in a sense, your Guru. They make sure that all of your attachments are visible. In reality, they are none other than an aspect of Self communicating wisdom to you.

Bring your reactivity onto your path.

When you find yourself reacting with tension to a difficult situation with another person in your community, apply your practice. While sometimes circumstances have to be talked through, the only permanent solution is to realize more.

Try to open your heart using the tools you have been given.

When you encounter difficult situations with people, don't plan "how to be" or "what to say" or "how to sound more compassionate." If you just do the nitty gritty work of opening your heart, whatever happens next will always be more skillful.

Being Together

8.
Changing
for Real

*The process of waking up will totally transform
your experience of your body, energy, and mind,
and yet you will discover what you have always
been all along.*

Tantra Fresh and Original

Changing for Real

One Thanksgiving eve, I dreamt that some old friends (a.k.a. old habits) were making a Thanksgiving feast, but I wasn't invited. Right in the middle of this dream, I began to experience intense pain in my chest and an intense feeling of grief. I was aware in the dream of the karmic nature of this pain. Even while feeling this pain to the maximum, I also had some perspective on it.

Doing sadhana enables one to have this kind of perspective, even in the midst of reactivity. So, at some point, I took a strong decision. I decided to leave the house of pain and go outside to explore.

Outside, everything was shimmering with fresh, vibrant life. I saw lakes and mountains and trails. Small birds and other animals frolicked in grass sparkling with new rain. People's faces were also eloquently expressive. At some point, I came upon a green, rolling park filled with diverse, beautiful animals. A tiger was running, its stripes flashing out from between the trees.

I had no particular place to go and no expectations. I was just exploring and enjoying. Everything that occurred was full of interest, intelligence, and immediacy.

There is freshness and originality to the situation of being alive and being aware in life. In order to experience this freshness and originality, we have to step out of karma. Karma means habit patterns — good or bad.

Frankly, though, most of us are firmly convinced that our habits are who we are. So we don't want to step out of them. From our limited perspective, stepping out of habit feels like dying. And it is a dying. As practitioners, having the courage to let old forms of life die is absolutely necessary. We have to cultivate this courage and revise our View of death.

When habit patterns are getting ready to die, they make a last stand. They become more intense. They feel all-encompassing as if we will never be able to escape from them. Part of maturing as a practitioner is being able to discern when this process of dying is occurring and to just keep going on with our practice, day-by-day. In due time, the pattern will pop and naturally dissolve.

The way to boldly step out of karma is not necessarily to attack your habit patterns or try to aggressively rout them out. Anandamayi Ma taught that there is no need to renounce anything. Everything that needs to fall away will fall away naturally under the gentle force of our sadhana. Be bold and just keep practicing no matter what. In this way, you can trade in your stale karmic patterns for immediacy and freshness.

Liberation Inch-by-Inch

Changing for Real

Perhaps you are somewhat disappointed that you've found no stories here of kundalini earthquakes, miracle healings, or siddhas who walk through walls. The stream of teachings you are encountering here is more like a workshop in somebody's backyard garage. As you walk by, you hear hammering and sawing, a bit of singing, and you wonder who is working so hard in there.

The fact is, when we read about amazing spiritual experiences or tales of dramatic breakthroughs, what we often don't glimpse are the years of simple, consistent sadhana that allowed those moments to arise. People with a high degree of perceptual openness have almost always done an enormous amount of practice. In fact, in the ancient Tantras, or written texts of my tradition, the most prized aspect of human life is that we possess bodies that can do so many kinds of sadhana. According to the tradition, human life is the sadhana-doing-realm.

Despite the allure of amazing spiritual experiences and "sudden realization," the process of spiritual growth for ninety-nine percent of us proceeds in small steps. If you want to keep going, you need to learn to recognize and take daily pleasure in the infinite textures of this unfolding.

When I started practicing, I didn't know "Tantra" was the name for what I was doing. I didn't know from which country or tradition the methods came. Later, when I did know and had found a teacher and a community, I had no thought of measuring my accomplishments against those of others. I had no idea how my experience stacked up to anyone else's. I also didn't read a lot of books detailing "amazing" experiences. I was more attracted to tales of disciples' devotion to their Gurus and to the poetry and teaching texts of Trika Shaivism.

I was much more likely to compete for the emotional attention of my teacher than for siddhis or marks of spiritual specialness. "Enlightenment" seem so lofty and far off, I hardly considered it. All I wanted to do was find out about reality. This had been the driving preoccupation of my life.

I practiced every day. For years on end. For hours and hours a day. Through a natural process and without planning, every moment of my life, waking, working, and sleeping, became sadhana.

It was through this steady, day-by-day, step-by-step process that some breakthroughs did occur, much to my surprise. But the greatest miracle has been the opening of the heart.

So don't fret if you haven't yet come across the secret, all-in-one liberation pill that everyone knows about but you. Inch-by-inch is the way.

9.
Finding the Magic

Impermanence is a spelling, a magical display, the glamour of the Absolute.

Get Real Magic

The difference between my students here in the U.S. and many of those who write to me from India is, in one respect, dramatic. Folks who write from India usually assume that I have powers such as clairvoyance and the ability to predict the future. I have been asked for mantras to manifest deities, magnetize someone's affections, and kill annoying neighbors.

Here in the U.S., I have to stuff skeptical students full of stories about the magic of the world. I tell them about accomplished human beings who walk through walls; become invisible; receive dream transmissions of complex practices; and see far off people, places, and things as if they were in the same room.

I try to impress upon my students that the sounds of kundalini running in the channels of a human body are more captivating than any rock concert, that the lights of the five elements are more entertaining than the latest science fiction blockbuster movie, and that just being in the world in a relaxed and natural way is a higher high than that offered by any drug.

I watch their faces and often see a mixture of uncertainty, cool cynicism, and longing.

Despite all of our whiz-bang technology, we live in a culture that is almost devoid of any comprehension of real magic. What do I mean by real magic?

I mean the manifest world experienced through senses which have opened and subtilized. I mean the fullness of reality revealing itself through someone in a human body. I mean the jewel-like display of creative overflow we call impermanence. I mean the magical correspondences between a human body and the cosmos. I mean the heart opening so that it becomes completely impossible not to feel love and devotion toward every being. I mean the eternal light of consciousness shining forth from it all.

Our parents, by and large, have not brought us up with tales of human beings who embody more of reality than ordinary mind can readily imagine. Most people in the U.S. do not actually know a single person of spiritual accomplishment. When we meet a human who has realized a fuller capacity, we categorize that person as being very different from us. We call that person a shaman or a reincarnation or a saint or crazy. We often suspect charlatanism.

We rarely entertain the possibility that the innate magic of reality can reveal itself to a human being whose only special power is the desire to do consistent spiritual practice. If we had more exposure to accomplished practitioners, we might develop more confidence in ourselves and in the process of awakening.

Many of the stories of spiritual accomplishment that we label as superstition or fantasy are actually more real than all of the crap we believe. Like that the world is solid; made up of distinct objects; explainable by scientific methods; and fixable by the right combination of life coaching, psychotherapy, designer pharmaceuticals, and cosmetic surgery.

I used to know an accomplished yogini from Tibet—Venerable Naljorma Jangchup Palmo. She passed away in 2014. Venerable Naljorma was a wonderful practitioner and teacher of Chöd. She told me that in Tibet, she never revealed to students what practices she had completed, nor did she speak of her experiences. Here, she said, she was more likely to do these things because students need it. She was acting out of compassion, not egoism.

Even when students in the West find an accomplished teacher, they sometimes cannot relax, feel transmission, or allow themselves time to let spiritual practice develop. They don't have any confidence in real magic, and so they won't risk setting out on the adventure of seeking it.

I always hope students will see me as an ordinary person who has practiced consistently for some years and has realized some of the fruits of that practice. First of all, this is the truth. Second of all, I want students to feel greater confidence in the process of life and the teachings of the tradition. If I tell them about some of the more "amazing" events in my life, it is not to appear special, but precisely because I am not special. If I can experience the world's magic just by doing consistent sadhana, so can anyone.

When you allow yourself to have confidence in the teacher, the teachings, reality, or yourself, you can relax and let yourself be carried along. You can be more open and exploratory. Then the real magic of life can appear before you, as you. You don't need to rid yourself of doubts. Doubting is a soft and open position. You do need to let go of the brittle blinders of skepticism and give magic a chance in spite of your fear of disappointment.

Take a look around. Find a teacher in whom you can see your real potential as a human being. Don't compromise on that. Then you can discover real magic for yourself.

Karma and Mercy

Finding the Magic

When we talk about karma, good or bad, we are talking about the responses of Nature to our activity in the world. If we repeatedly eat improperly, we get sick. Our emotions and mind become unbalanced. If we repeatedly spend money improperly, we get into financial trouble. If we are repeatedly angry and rude, people won't want to spend time with us. If we repeatedly do sadhana, there are a host of other kinds of responses. This is the simplest way of understanding karma, but of course there is more to it than these simple examples.

Karma does not refer to a mechanical process of cause and effect as is sometimes taught. Karma is the multi-faceted, multidimensional conversation that God is having with the creation. It is more like call and response.

Repeated actions create patterns that persist in time and engender responses. These responses are not punishments. They actually contain within them wisdom seeds that can help us to realize even if it is by becoming totally sick of ourselves or literally sick. Other responses, such as to us doing consistent sadhana, we call "good karma." But in a relative sense, all karma is wisdom.

Each being has what is called *prarabdha karma*. Prarabdha is that portion of one's total karma that is set to ripen in a particular lifetime. But it may have begun forming in any time and place. So, for instance, the shape of your life is partially created by activities and responses set in motion long ago. You also carry and help to shape family, national, human, gender, ethnic, and other karmas.

When we are mostly sleep-walking through our lives, severely limited by our small sense of self, we are unaware of the responsivity of the world to our actions. We cannot hear the world communicating to us. We are compulsive and reactive instead of naturally responsive.

This is very easy to understand in an everyday way. Some people can feel their way gracefully and skillfully through complex situations in life. Other people are always bumping into obstacles because they cannot see the open door. But if we bump into a closed door numerous times, we eventually stop and try to open it before proceeding.

As we continue on the path, we inevitably become attuned to the more subtle nuances of the world communication. We can notice responses immediately and adjust our activity. Over time, we learn that a misstep can be corrected in a moment by opening one's heart and yielding to wisdom. We always get infinite chances to open our senses, open our hearts, and act more wisely. Reality never gives up on us. This is the definition of mercy.

This alive, aware reality gives us instantaneous feedback in every moment. It can be quite magical. One time, when I had just started to teach, I over-committed myself by promising to offer a series of workshops at a prominent yoga studio. My enthusiasm and pride got the better of me. I felt important. Later I realized that the job was a misuse of my energy. This realization happened in Whole Foods Market.

I found myself pushing my cart down an aisle, spontaneously asking my Guru Anandamayi Ma to get me out of this new karmic entanglement. I was entirely focused on my internal conversation with Ma. Just then, my phone rang. It was the owner of the yoga studio. She suggested that we put the workshops off as the studio schedule was already quite full. As you can imagine, I readily agreed.

This process has repeated many times. Through it, I have learned directly that the possibility to surrender our limitations, relax, and realize is always present, even in the darkest of circumstances. We are always guided devotedly by a world Self that is our eternal home, our true Guru, and our compassionate Mother. Our job is to try to find a way to offer ourselves at the feet of the world.

Comfort, Salvation, Burning, and Melting

Many people desire experiences that soften their feelings of anxiety and isolation. We search for these experiences in sex, food, drugs, relationships, and in our spiritual practice. The desire to feel more comfortable being alive is probably the number one reason people seek teachings.

People of all faiths, and even atheists, long to be saved. The desire to be saved attracts a lot of people to lineages in which teachers promise miracles, tout "sudden enlightenment, or give shaktipat. This desire fuels attachment to stories of amazing spiritual feats. People can become spiritual experience junkies just as they can become sugar or heroin addicts.

Seeking miracles or wanting someone else to cause us to become enlightened can be great obstacles. Sometimes these kinds of desires keep us from beginning any kind of practice. But if we *do* practice, the combination of stubbornness and frustration can eventually force us to get more real and gain more confidence in the incremental, coming and going way of waking up.

We can begin to take more responsibility for our journey. We become capable of working with a teacher and of relating to the teachings in a more mature way. We develop a higher capacity for self-reflection, and our reactivity to the circumstances of our lives begins to diminish.

At some point, we begin to work very hard. We desperately desire to fully unfold within ourselves the courage and capacity to discover our real nature. This is the "burning" stage. It can last many years or even lifetimes.

When I finally read Yogananda's *Autobiography of a Yogi* at the age of forty-five, I was deep in the stage of effortful sadhana. I felt desperate for insight into the nature of reality, my nature. I am talking about real desperation. The kind that hurts your heart and leaves you gasping for breath.

What struck me most about the story occurred near the end. The narrator is granted visions of accomplished beings who have moved on to other, non-earthly realms and who are still doing sadhana to help them unwind remaining karmas.[13] I felt, not excitement, but a sense of horror. Was I going to be at this for eons? Painstakingly untying the knots in age after age, realm after realm?

Later, though, desperation begins to soften. We find ourselves in less of a life and death struggle with our limitations. We discover a new, quieter sense of intimacy with life. The distinctions between "inside" and "outside" begin to dissolve. We no longer experience our teachers or other wisdom beings as radically different from ourselves. When we hear the voices of our teachers, we hear our own wisdom speaking to us.

Eventually we realize that the entire world is a living communication of Self to Self. There is nothing to pursue or collect. The individualistic "I" we thought was on the road to being rewarded for all of that hard work is discovered to be itself a limiting concept.

The understanding dawns that there are infinite factors involved in the process of waking up. Our sadhana is one factor, but it is not all up to us. We are letting go of even the identity of "yogi," or whatever our spiritual identity happens to be. Attachment is just attachment,

Finding the Magic

and any attachments will hold you back. Even the attachment to conceiving of yourself as a "practitioner."

Now I find it impossible to experience the life process as so burdensome. I no longer experience horror at the thought of myself soldiering on alone toward enlightenment. Not that I am enlightened. I'm just not so much of a soldier and not so alone.

In my earlier years, I tried to push through to greater realization. Now I am listening. I am using my freedom to follow life, to follow nature, to follow the promptings of wisdom. Devotion has largely usurped struggle. Melting has replaced burning. I now understand the value of patience, humility, and modesty. This result is somewhat funny, but also somewhat of a miracle—just not the sort of miracle I anticipated when I first set out.

What is Grace?

We all have expectations of ourselves, others, and the world that are based on our tensions—on our limited View of what is possible for us and life.

Someone suggests: Why don't you try this new way of doing things? A person might habitually answer: Oh no, that will never work!

This is an example of a common kind of limitation of View. The person wonders why new opportunities never seem to arise when they were in fact refusing them day after day.

We have many entrenched Views of ourselves and others. We are so enslaved by these that we don't even notice when life surprises us. We may dismiss a circumstance that doesn't fit our story. We actually enjoy getting right back to our miserable outlook. We condemn ourselves and others to narrow, painful roles in life. In this condition, we are like jars with the lids on. Little nourishment or learning can get through to us.

When we begin to practice in a spiritual tradition, we slowly let go of our defense of our self-image. We start to notice more about ourselves and other people. The world begins to come alive again. Skepticism, negativity, and anxiety start to be relieved by moments of relaxation and natural enjoyment. In this new condition brought about by consistent effort in sadhana, we can notice life responding to us and assisting us. We can continue with renewed dedication and desire.

A student of mine recently had this experience. She was involved in a situation with another person that had been stuck for quite some time. Her View was that she couldn't do anything but continue to be entangled. She was already projecting her negativity a year into the future when she was certain that she would not be able to go on a planned pilgrimage to India with me because of this other person.

However, through her sadhana and listening to the teachings, she gained more clarity about her role in keeping the entanglement going. She gained enough detachment to resolve to change her behavior in a significant way. Still, karmic tensions were expressing as a certainty that the other person would respond badly to her desire to go to India with me.

What happened instead was that the other person, upon hearing her new clarity and resolve, did something "surprising." He offered to pay for her trip. Now this student has more opportunity to practice and more confidence in life.

This is a manifestation of grace. We experience a sudden opening to a new level of opportunity that comes about as a response to our effort. When we are 100 percent ready to resolve some karmic tension, that is entirely the same as God being 100 percent ready. Self responds to the Self-surrender of Self.

That we are rarely 100 percent ready to give up our attachments to habits of body, energy, and mind is why waking up takes so darn long! But it is also why it could take only an instant.

When we start to relax, we more and more notice how life is supporting us to continue our practice. This "support" can come in the form of challenges and restraints, but we discover that it is all grace. Whatever happens has the potential to move us in the

Finding the Magic

direction of deeper relaxation and clarity.

When I left my academic job, I decided not to look for work. I decided to throw myself into the arms of life and just see what happened. This decision was based on my longing to participate in the ancient practice from India of spending time wandering with no home and no means of support other than the generosity and wisdom of the world at large. You leave your home with nothing other than your clothing. You don't ask for money or lodging or food. You see what happens.

Of course, my form of this practice was not at all severe. I had just quit a fancy academic position. I had lots of possessions and enough money to get an apartment! But some people still thought I was crazy. And I was still surprised that from the moment I made my decision, people offered me writing work. I spent three years doing intensive sadhana, working just enough to pay the bills, and never asking for anything other than what came my way. Even this comparatively safe experiment taught me a lot about the natural collaboration between practitioners and reality.

Other aspects of the human experience of grace can be more spectacular. These are the kinds of manifestations of spiritual accomplishment that you read about or perhaps have experienced yourself. A teacher gives a mantra in a dream. Or an "incurable" illness is resolved through prayer. Or you experience a time when a more realized condition visits to show you the way. Or you meet your real teacher. That is supreme grace.

Whatever it is, you can be sure that you are being responded to because of your readiness. Now, having that response, it is time to stabilize the insights and effects of that experience. An experience of grace is never a culmination. It is an invitation to realize more and a new beginning.

10.
Living from
the Heart

*The heart of reality that is everywhere and the cave
of the heart in the center of a human being are one
fountain of wisdom eternally joyful
and overflowing.*

A Habitable Life

The sole purpose of human life is to self-realize. When we do practice, after a time we discover that this purpose was built-in all along. In fact, waking up is so ingrained in us, it's hardly correct to call that a "purpose." Our myriad spiritual paths are just nature accomplishing itself. You don't need any additional justification for your life.

This doesn't mean that we should drop everything and head for remote mountain caves. The fundamental insight of direct realization householder traditions is that we can discover essence nature in any situation if we do not allow ourselves to get too distracted by karmic patterns. The divine is immanent in manifest life. Everything we need to realize is right here, in our own bodies and in ordinary circumstance.

If we are to be householders, we must eat and take basic care of ourselves and our dependents. Most of us are engaged in some kind of work. We also enjoy friends, family, and cultures.

As householder practitioners, it is desirable to establish what I call "a habitable life." A habitable life is one in which we have cultivated the circumstances most conducive to helping us wake up.

Here are three guidelines for creating a life that supports your practice.

Find something to do that makes a positive contribution, that you enjoy, and that leaves you enough energy to keep doing your practice and participating in non-work aspects of life.

Try not to over-identify with what you do to earn money. Your job is to self-realize. You've had that job since you were conceived, and you'll never be laid off!

Carry out your responsibilities with an attitude of simplicity, practicality, and positivity.

Don't make a big deal out of life's duties. Approach circumstances that arise with the practical question: How can I work with this? Appreciate each circumstance as an opportunity to relax and grow. Enjoy the rhythms of each day and try not to overdo.

Make your daily practice and remembering your true nature the main "business" of your life.

Integrate practices such as mantra and Guru Yoga into your everyday activities. Try to remain immersed in presence and open your heart.

Ahimsa and Devotion

Ahimsa, or nonviolence, is often interpreted as "not killing" or "not hurting" others. But how can we possibly avoid hurting others when we are busy harming ourselves? In fact, how can we avoid harming others when we are not even aware of the myriad ways in which we harm ourselves at every moment?

Direct realization traditions teach us that establishing ourselves with awareness in the natural state is the foundation upon which we can live a life of ahimsa or non-harming. So we must tend to our own liberation first before we can entertain the idea that we know what is good for others.

The original "harm" is our fervent conviction that we are separate from others, that we possess an "I" distinct from all else. This small I insists on defending its feeling of having boundaries, and this insistence drives the compulsions and habits we call normal life.

All of our defensive, repetitive thoughts and behaviors are geared toward reinforcing small I. The more we relax through the process of sadhana, the more these patterns of compulsion stand out in relief and the more we notice how they control our lives. Without this awareness, painful as it may be, we are living in a fog through which both ourselves and others are only dimly visible.

But we are not helpless. We can refrain from gross harms against ourselves and others by following precepts laid out for us by our cultures, families, teachers, and traditions. We can do our best, given our limited understanding, to minimize harm in a conventional way. There is nothing wrong with this course of action, as long as we do not mistake it for a more profound embodiment of ahimsa.

That *ahimsa* reveals itself first as an encounter with our own indestructible value. We are born of and made of awareness, energy, and wisdom. Our *vajra* (adamantine) nature is good without an opposite. It shines with unfettered intelligence and joy. Recognizing this, even partially, is the beginning of true ahimsa.

When we begin to touch this, a feeling of devotion and caring simultaneously arises. We have experiential knowledge of what we really are, and this knowledge is equal to, or inevitably gives rise to, devotion. The direct knowledge of Self blooms into a sincere desire to benefit everyone along with the capacity to spontaneously and skillfully embody that benefit through our activities.

Sometimes people think that one kind of tradition is devotional while another isn't. The fact is that any path you follow through to the end will lead you to discover devotion, because devotion is immanent in the nature of reality. There is no realization without the discovery of devotion.

Many of the teachers of the various Tantrik traditions that flourished from the 5th to 12th centuries in Kashmir were highly-educated intellectuals. They engaged with gusto in debates with their peers and wrote about art, drama, and philosophy. They also produced some of the greatest devotional hymns and poetry known to humankind. In fact, I have observed that the more realized one becomes, the more devotional one's writings, practice, and mode of teaching becomes.

No matter where you begin, devotion is everyone's destination in the end because your real nature is made of devotion and wisdom.

Living from the Heart

When you come to know your Self, you understand that the whole creation is expressing devotion toward itself. You become immersed in the ocean of natural devotion. Everything you do expresses that.

Living from the Heart

You Can Always Serve

No matter in what condition you find yourself, you can always serve. No matter how low you feel about yourself, even if your life is falling apart, you can always contribute by serving others. For this reason, service is the great refuge.

You may hear your teacher say that you should take refuge in your own nature. You might feel that you don't have this capacity. You may not yet even understand what that means. But you don't have to be highly realized to take refuge in service. What a wonderful circumstance!

People have various feelings about *seva* (service to teacher and community) and *karma yoga* (service to anyone on a regular basis). When I was much younger, I used to call seva, "slave-a." Now, I am so happy to be able to serve in any moment, in every moment.

When I am offering service, there is no need to fight with myself or tackle complicated "problems." I don't have to worry about anything or try to accomplish anything difficult. I can just serve.

You can cook a meal, wash a window, or weed a garden. You can lend a hand with shopping. You can clean something or teach someone. You can run an errand. You can offer a kind word or a kindly listen. In any moment, in every moment, you can offer service to your teacher, to your teacher's family, to your community, to your friends, or to a stranger.

When you are taking refuge in service, you can access a tremendous feeling of gratitude for at least being able to serve despite all of your other limitations. Maybe you can't practice for hours or at all. Maybe you can't study texts. Maybe you are crabby or sad or awkward. But you can serve. Gratitude for this simple vehicle for getting in touch with your own goodness is the *mahabhava* (great attitude) of all real service.

Sometimes you hear people talk about "selfless service." They mean serving without any attachment to getting something in return, including admiration or thanks. What I mean by taking refuge in service is a somewhat different orientation to serving.

Taking refuge in service, you realize that we are all in the same boat. You need refuge from all of your inner and outer machinations. When you are serving, you can just focus on that activity and feel satisfied with yourself. When you are satisfied—feeling your simple, essential goodness as you serve—that feeling is automatically shared with others.

By serving, everyone feels, at least a bit, that samsara is okay. Life is not so much of a burden. We can express simple care toward ourselves and each other by performing these little acts. Even during the worst of times, we can be reminded of our goodness and our capacity for caring for each other. What a relief!

The best aspect of service is that, with each simple act, you actually *are* taking refuge in your own nature. The fundamental nature of God is devotional. The dance of service is God's dance, and it is also your dance.

Living from the Heart

Destination Open Heart

We have three experiences of body: a physical body experience, an energy body experience, and a wisdom body experience. Each of these is a different version or aspect of the other.

All people can experience the physical body in some way or another. Some people have a more tangible experience of subtle energy. For instance, some people can sense the emotions of others. Sensing the emotions of others involves physical cues, but it can also involve feeling energetic states. Others can feel energy moving in their subtle channels or even direct their subtle energy.

Most people also have contact with their wisdom body, if only intermittently. When you are presented with a choice, and you have an instantaneous upsurge of certain knowledge about which direction you should choose, that is often a communication from your wisdom body. It could also be that, through a combination of anxiety, caffeine, and over-enthusiasm, you've superseded wisdom and are just following compulsion.

You can tell the difference easily. Following wisdom might be a little scary, but it always results in relaxation. Following compulsion leads to more compulsion. Nothing is resolved.

Traditions that invoke some relationship to Indian Tantra tend to overemphasize the energy body in their descriptions of practices and accomplishments. This is particularly true when these traditions are exported out of their original contexts. The control of energy, the energetic aspects of transmission experiences, and spectacular energy "events" are valorized and celebrated. Kundalini experiences are described in mostly energetic terms. But it is the wisdom body that gives rise to both the energy body and the physical body.

Unlike the physical and energy bodies, the wisdom body is not karmically conditioned or constrained. For this reason, the spontaneous upsurge of incontrovertible knowing does not always follow "the rules" of conventional life. If we do not recognize our wisdom, or it scares us, we block it with various karmically infused and more familiar modes of thinking, feeling, and behaving. This is conditioning.

The goal of direct realization practice is to live immersed in natural wisdom and to spontaneously follow wisdom. Just having various energetic experiences is not enough!

Because we live in an information-mad culture, we may not realize that the word "wisdom" refers to anything other than some pontifications about life. This is not at all the case.

Wisdom here means the stuff of which reality is composed: primordial intelligence, self-reflectivity, creativity, compassion, clarity, curiosity, and mercy. So, I like to say "wisdom virtue" instead of just "wisdom."

The wisdom virtues are pervasive and fundamental. They don't belong to anyone, although they show up in individuals. They also cannot be cultivated because they are complete and perfect already. We can remove the obscurations that prevent wisdom virtues from showing up in full measure in our bodies, energy, and minds.

One symbol brings together all of these virtues: the heart. The heart is the fountain-like center of reality from which manifestations continuously overflow impelled by pure expressive joy. This heart is everywhere.

In a human being, the living symbol of the heart of reality is the heart chakra, *anahata chakra*, or more generally an area in the center of the chest. This is sometimes called the heart center or the cave of the heart. It is not the physical heart.

The heart center is a *sandhi*, a juncture or a gap through which human beings directly experience primordial wisdom and the universalization of all virtues. When the heart center is functioning in a more realized way, we experience uncaused, unconditioned love for everyone. We overflow with uncaused, unconditioned compassion for everyone. We experience all manifestations as aspects of our own body, energy, and mind. Our lives are a free-flowing expression of the natural devotion of Self to Self.

This total intimacy and open-heartedness is the real destination of all direct realization sadhana.

11.
Crossing Over

Do you start to wail and cry if a person goes to another room in the house? This death is inevitably connected with this life. In the sphere of Immortality, where is the question of death and loss? Nobody is lost to me.[14]

—Anandamayi Ma

Messages from Another Room

I can barely remember Dayavati before she got cancer. We had the same spiritual teacher for some years. But we didn't become close right away. As her life drew to a close, we spoke weekly or even more frequently.

Dayavati was born in Jamaica, but lived in Toronto for many years. She developed triple negative cancer, a drug-resistant cancer that is more prevalent in people of African descent. Most of our conversations were about spiritual practice. During the last six months of her life, we talked about dying as a practitioner.

Like the rest of us, Dayavati's strengths both helped her and got her into trouble. And her troubles often led her back to herself and her practice.

She was courageous and stubborn. Persevering and fearful. Big-hearted and demanding. Vibrant, vivacious, and ruefully attached to food that was not helpful to her.

Above all, Dayavati was a practitioner, but not the kind of practitioner you read about in books. She was like most of us: chipping away at fears and fixations day-by-day, zooming ahead, waffling, taking detours, running around in circles, finding her ground, making excuses, courageously facing the truth, and then forgetting it again until next time.

Dayavati loved her teachers, and she loved Anandamayi Ma. Even though she buckled down to daily practice only in the last two years of her life, she truly understood and embodied devotion. She had a spectacular, unwavering, devoted heart.

The cancer, however, was aggressive and wily: a karmic juggernaut.

After many surgeries; rounds of radiation and chemo; and visits to expert acupuncturists, naturopaths, and healers, the cancer spread. It took both breasts; fractured Dayavati's spine; and invaded her liver, lungs, and brain.

Dayavati passed into the bardos on Monday, December 1, 2008. She was surrounded by friends, sangha, and family. She was fifty-two years old.

The last time I spoke to Dayavati, she could no longer move, eat, or drink. Edema had crept into her abdomen. Breath was decreasing. She spoke only an occasional single word.

She was withdrawing, preserving whatever strength she had for the transition.

Her sister kindly held the phone to Dayavati's ear. I told Dayavati that her entire spiritual community worldwide was holding her in their hearts and practicing for her.

In a voice so depleted of prana, I could barely make out her words, she said: *I feel it. Thank you.*

I spoke a few other words, mainly encouraging her to relax. And then I reminded her that she could do Guru Yoga, and I repeated Om Ma several times. This was a mantra Dayavati loved.

She then began saying, over and over again in a more distinct voice: *I remember, I remember, I remember.*

There was a note of childlike wonder, even happiness, as if she had indeed forgotten and was glad to rediscover something so familiar and fundamental.

Crossing Over

Every practitioner works to remember the habit of practice during the transits of death and the bardos. I felt reassured and deeply moved.

In the way that she lived and died, Dayavati left us with many profound messages to reflect upon.

The first message is this. No matter how, as practitioners, we struggle to stay on the path, no matter what our so-called failings or lapses—and we all experience these in abundance—keeping on, until the time of death, remembering, remembering, remembering, and remembering again is a great victory. A great, great victory.

So, *Jai Jai Jai* Dayavati Sarasvati!

You will never be lost.

Crossing Over

Endnotes

1. Anandamayi Ma, "Ma in Her Words," privately circulated PDF, multiple translators and sources, 28.

2. Abhinavagupta, *Gitartha Samgraha, Abhinavagupta's Commentary on the Bhagavad Gita*, trans. Boris Marjanovic (Varanasi: Indica Books, 2002), 107-47.

3. Anandamayi Ma, "Matri Vani," *Ananda Varta*, Shree Shree Anandamayee Sangha, Varanasi, Vol. IV:1, 1956: 59.

4. Abhinavagupta, 5.

5. Quoted in Richard Lannoy, *Anandamayi: Her Life and Wisdom*, (Rockport, MA: Element, 1996), 8.

6. Ram Kumar Rai, *Kularnava Tantra*, (Varanasi: Prachya Prakashan, 1983), 251.

7. Anandamayi Ma, *Words of Sri Anandamayi Ma*, trans. Atmananda (Haridwar: Shree Shree Anandamayee Sangha Kankhal, 2008), 3.

8. Anandamayi Ma, "Sri Sri Ma's Utterances," *Ananda Varta*, Shree Shree Anandamayee Sangha, Varanasi, Vol. XXXIV:1, 1987: 3.

9. Vicki Mackenzie, *Cave in the Snow: Tenzin Palmo's Quest for Enlightenment*, (New York: Bloomsbury Paperbacks, 1998), 144.

10. Anandamayi Ma, *Words of Sri Anandamayi Ma,* trans. Atmananda (Haridwar: Shree Shree Anandamayee Sangha Kankhal, 2008), 89.

11. "Knowledge is bondage" is the second sutra of the first section of *The Shiva Sutras* by Vasgupta. Vasgupta, *The Aphorisms of Siva: The Sivasutra with Bhaskara's Commentary, the Varttika,* trans. with exposition and notes by Mark S. G. Dyczkowski, (Albany: State University of New York Press, 1992), 15.

12. Alexis Sanderson, "The Śaiva Exegesis of Kashmir," *Mélanges tantriques à la mémoire d'Hélène Brunner: Tantric Studies in Memory of Hélène Brunner,* edited by Dominic Goodall and André Padoux, (Pondicherry: IFI / EFEO, 2007), 327.

13. Paramahansa Yogananda, *Autobiography of a Yogi,* (Los Angeles: Self-Realization Fellowship, 1988), 352-69.

14. Anandamayi Ma, quoted on http://www.anandamayi.org/introduction-to-sri-mas-life/, Retrieved on August 21, 2018.

Endnotes

Alphabetical List of Titles

Alphabetical List of Titles

Acknowledgments

Many thanks to Shaka McGlotten for his generous editorial assistance and to Matridarshana Lamb for the same and for supporting Jaya Kula Press to disseminate the teachings. Thanks to Ambika Beber for all she does to support Jaya Kula Press. Thanks also to my students and the larger Jaya Kula community. Their sincere efforts to wake up and the questions they ask along the way have shaped much of the writing offered here.

About Jaya Kula Press

Jaya Kula Press is a project of Jaya Kula, a registered 501(c)3 nonprofit organization headquartered in Portland, Maine.

Jaya Kula Press supports dharma practitioners by presenting spiritual teachings that are precise, practical, faithful to their origins, and yet accessible to a wide range of people.

We currently publish the teachings of Shambhavi Sarasvati, the spiritual director of Jaya Kula.

About Jaya Kula

Jaya Kula is a vibrant, nonprofit householder community offering opportunities to learn and practice in the direct realization traditions of Trika Shaivism and Dzogchen. Our centers are in the Portlands: Maine and Oregon.

Made in the USA
Monee, IL
16 January 2022

89126068R00111